HOW TO TROUBLE YOUR TROUBLE

by

Creflo A. Dollar, Jr.

HARRISON HOUSE
Tulsa, Oklahoma

How to Trouble Your Trouble
ISBN 1-57794-061-X
Copyright © 1998 by Dr. Creflo A. Dollar Jr.
Creflo Dollar Ministries
2500 Burdette Road
College Park, Georgia 30349

Published by Harrison House, Inc.
P. O. Box 35035
Tulsa, Oklahoma 74153

Contents

Preface

SUPERNATURAL OR SHOWBOAT?

O n the Sunday morning I began preaching the series of sermons which is the basis for this book, God gave me a startling assignment. "Be sure," He said, "your people understand the difference between living in the supernatural and living on Showboat." Now I thought the term *showboat* was a strange one for God to use, but I realized I knew what He meant. He meant that to live in the supernatural does not require an emotional demonstration of the spectacular. *To live in the supernatural only requires that the Word of God works for you when you do it.*

Living in the supernatural means that you can take the "super" of God and apply it to your natural circumstances and situations — and get results. To live a life getting results from God's Word and winning is living in the supernatural. To expect anything other than that is to expect the wrong thing. It's ludicrous to expect that when God pours out His glory and a great anointing upon the earth, all of a sudden we are all going to start flying around and doing unusual or unnatural things. A person who is living in the supernatural is one who can say, "I live in this natural world, but I'm winning because of the 'super' of God."

Getting Results

How can you tell if you're truly living in the supernatural and not just in some counterfeit "showboat" experience where there may be lots of shouting and singing and dancing, and lots of spectacular events which seem to be manifestations of God's power? The answer is — you're living in the supernatural *if you are consistently getting results from God's Word.*

Child of God, you are living a supernatural life if you're praying prayers and your prayers are being answered. If you're confessing the Word and you can see what you say. If you're laying hands on the sick and the sick are being healed. If you're standing in faith for your finances and finances are being added to you. Don't let the spectacular manifestations mislead you into thinking that if an experience is not a "showboat" experience, it is not supernatural. A supernatural experience is not necessarily spectacular. An experience is supernatural when the "super" of God is manifested in your life so that the result is manifested in your life. Supernatural living is getting results from the Word of God and winning through all the tests and trials and adverse circumstances of your natural life.

To put it the other way, if you're not getting results from God's Word, you're not living supernaturally. If you go to church every time the doors are open, shout, scream, dance, sing, prophesy and speak in tongues, but when you go home you're still sick, you're still broke, you're still in bondage, your marriage is still on the rocks, you're not living in the supernatural. No matter how many exciting and spectacular things happen during the church service, if you can't apply what you hear about the Word of God to your life when you get home, you're not living supernaturally. You're living in defeat.

But if, on the other hand, you don't experience anything emotionally exciting or spectacular while you're at church, but when you get home, you can apply the teaching you've heard from the Word of God to your own circumstances, you are living in the supernatural. You are living the supernatural life God intended for

His children to live because you are getting results and living in victory through the Word of God.

The Spectacular Will Come

And don't worry that living in the supernatural rather than merely in the spectacular is going to doom you to a boring life. What could be boring about getting results from the Word of God? And when we all begin living supernaturally the way God wants us to live, the emotions and the spectacular manifestations will come when we assemble ourselves together to praise and worship God and to share our testimonies. The emotions will rise when I'm at home getting results, and you're at home getting results and someone else is at home getting results. When everyone in the congregation is getting results from the Word of God, we're all going to shout and sing and dance when we get to church.

We're going to shout when we get together because somebody got healed this week. Somebody got a bill paid this week. Somebody got delivered this week. Somebody was saved from an automobile accident this week. Somebody didn't die this week, even though the doctors said they would. We're going to shout because marriages are working on account of the Word. We're going to dance and sing because finances are working on account of the Word of God. We're going to praise God because the "super" of God has brought people who were in bondage out into the supernatural life of freedom. We're going to get excited and emotional and shout about the goodness of the Lord because people who were formerly living in defeat are now living in victory.

Living in victory — that's what living in the supernatural is all about. That's what every sermon, every teaching on the Word of God should enable you to do. And that's my purpose in this book. In the pages that follow, I'm going to teach you how to use the weapons God has given us in His Word to overcome trouble in your life.

In Section I, "Troubling Your Trouble," I'll show you how to use the benefits of your status as a born-again child of God to put down deep roots in God's Word so that your life will bear fruit. Then I'll teach you how to use the forces of peace, joy and love to overcome every form of trouble the devil tries to bring against you.

In Section II, "Walking in the Confidence of God in Troubled Times," I'll show you how to maintain your victory and continue to live in the supernatural even in times of testing, trial and tribulation.

Throughout the book, I'll show you from the Word that just because trouble comes, it doesn't have to overcome! And long before you finish the last chapter, I expect the Word of God to produce supernatural results in every area of your life. When you've truly learned to trouble your trouble, every time trouble shows up you will be able to say with Paul:

Our light affliction, which is but for a moment, worketh for us a far more exceeding and eternal weight of glory.

2 CORINTHIANS 4:17

Section I:
Troubling Your Trouble

Section I: Troubling Your Trouble

INTRODUCTION:
JUST BECAUSE TROUBLE COMES,
IT DOESN'T HAVE TO OVERCOME!

Some Christians seem to have the mistaken idea that just because they have been spiritually born again and translated out of the kingdom of darkness and into the kingdom of light (Colossians 1:13), they shouldn't have any more trouble in the world. Even though it's obvious that they've been troubled by trouble so long they don't think they'll ever get out of it, they put on an air of false cheerfulness. They exclaim, "Oh, Brother Dollar, since I've been born again, I haven't had any more trouble."

Well, my brother, my sister, what kind of "born-again" did you get? It couldn't have been the same one I got because when I got born again, I was introduced to a smorgasbord of trouble. When I got born again, trouble jumped on me before I even got out to the parking lot. Until I learned how to trouble my trouble and over-come it with the Word of God, I stayed in trouble. And from my experience as a pastor and teacher, I know that most Christians have just as much trouble with trouble as I did.

However, we shouldn't be surprised that trouble continues to trouble us even after we're born again. Jesus told us that as long as we're in this world we will have trouble.

> **These things I have spoken unto you, that in me ye might have peace. In the world ye shall have tribulation: but be of good cheer; I have overcome the world.**

> **JOHN 16:33**

In the world, Jesus said, you will have tribulation or trouble. But **in Me** you will have peace. Peace is security in the midst of trouble or turmoil. And where does peace come from? Jesus said peace comes from the words **I have spoken unto you.** So peace — security in the midst of turmoil — comes from the Word. In the world you will have trouble, but in the Word you will have peace.

Jesus and His Word are one. Therefore, He is saying here that although you live in the world where trouble is, you can stay secure by staying in the Word. As a born again child of God, you are still *in* this world physically, but you are not *of the system of this world*. That is, you do not operate or live your life according to the system of this world. You operate according to *the system of the Word of God.*

We are charged by the Scriptures to live in the Word of God. Yes, we are still in the world where trouble is, but we don't have to be troubled by trouble because Jesus said **I have overcome the world** system. How did Jesus overcome the world system? With the Word.

Now the good news is this — if Jesus overcame trouble, you can overcome trouble. Just because trouble comes, it doesn't have to overcome! As long as you are in this world, trouble will show up, but that doesn't mean you have to let it manifest itself in your life. You can learn to trouble your trouble so it won't be able to trouble you.

Of course, learning how to trouble your trouble is not instantaneous or automatic. All the trouble in your life will not necessarily disappear the minute you finish reading this book. But if you are diligent to find out who you are in Christ, to study the Word and to put down deep roots in it, and if you practice in your everyday life what I'm teaching you, the Word of God will bear fruit in your life. You will get results. When you learn to apply the Word to your trouble, trouble will have to flee. And then you will no longer be living in the world where there is tribulation and defeat, but in the Word where there is peace and victory.

1

CLUB *SOTERIA*

In order to trouble our trouble, we have to know, first of all, who we are in Christ and what has been made available to us in our position as born-again children of God. The book of Hebrews describes who we are and what our position is now that we're born again.

> And, Thou, Lord, in the beginning hast laid the foundation of the earth; and the heavens are the works of thine hands:
>
> They shall perish; but thou remainest; and they all shall wax old as doth a garment;
>
> And as a vesture shalt thou fold them up, and they shall be changed: but thou art the same, and thy years shall not fail.
>
> But to which of the angels said he at any time, Sit on my right hand, until I make thine enemies thy footstool?
>
> Are they not all ministering spirits, sent forth to minister for them who shall be heirs of salvation?
>
> Therefore we ought to give the more earnest heed to the things which we have heard, lest at any time we should let them slip.
>
> For if the word spoken by angels was stedfast, and every transgression and disobedience received a just recompence of reward;

How shall we escape, if we neglect so great salvation; which at the first began to be spoken by the Lord, and was confirmed unto us by them that heard him;

God also bearing them witness, both with signs and wonders, and with divers miracles, and gifts of the Holy Ghost, according to his own will?

For unto the angels hath he not put in subjection the world to come, whereof we speak.

But one in a certain place testified, saying, What is man, that thou art mindful of him? or the son of man, that thou visitest him?

HEBREWS 1:10-14; 2:1-6

In these verses God is establishing divine rank and order amongst Himself, men and angels. He makes clear the order of priority. Of course, He is the head, but He emphasizes that the rank that comes after God is not angels but man. Man ranks after God. Man has been given the invitation to come sit with Him in heavenly places in the anointed Jesus (Ephesians 2:6).

But concerning angels, the Scripture says they have been *sent forth* to minister *for* them who shall be heirs of salvation. Now, if God *sent* angels forth, they are anointed to do the job because any time God sends someone to do something, they are anointed to do the job He sent them to do. So we can be sure angels have a mission. They have a certain job to do. The Bible says the specific purpose of angels here on planet earth is to *minister* that is, to *serve* not just *to* some group of people but to minister *for* them. And who are they ministering for? The *heirs of salvation.*

Now, who are heirs? They are people who are in the position to inherit something. Something has been left for them; something is available to them. Something has been provided for them, and they now have the opportunity to get hold of it or take possession of it. Well, what is it the Bible says has been left for these heirs? What are they going to inherit? *Salvation.*

Salvation Versus *Born Again*

We have to be careful in using the word *salvation* because it has been confused in some religious circles with the term *born again*, even though these two terms are not synonymous. They are related ideas, but they do not mean exactly the same thing.

To be *born again* is what happens to your spirit after you repent, confess with your mouth the Lord Jesus Christ and believe in your heart that God raised Him from the dead. To be born again means you move from darkness into light. So, being born again involves a transition or translation from one point to another point, from one position to another position, based on a decision that you make.

However, *salvation* is what is available to you when you get born again. And it is not just something that's stored up in heaven for you in the "sweet by and by." It's not something you have to leave the earth in the Rapture to get. No. Salvation is what you have available to you right here and now as a born-again person. The word *salvation* in the New Testament comes from the Greek word *soteria*[1] which means *healing, safety, deliverance, protection, soundness* and includes with it the ministry of angels.

Therefore, God is saying that angels have been sent to serve the heirs of *soteria.* They have the responsibility of serving you if you're a born-again person. The angels are to serve you in the areas of healing, deliverance, safety, protection, soundness.

And they are to minister to you in any other areas where you have need.

Join the Club

Let me use an analogy to make clear what I mean by the difference between salvation and being born again.

Getting born again and becoming an heir of salvation is like joining a club. When you make a decision to join a club and have gone through the procedure of becoming a member, you are then entitled to use the club's facilities and have available to you all the benefits of membership. If, for instance, you make a decision to get in shape and join a fitness club, you then have available to you all the exercise equipment that particular club has to offer. You can work out on the circuit machines, swim in the pool, play handball in the handball courts, join an aerobics class. In other words, you can use whatever the club has available to help you get in shape.

The same thing is true when you get born again and join "Club *Soteria*." As a member of Club *Soteria* you have available to you the "stairmaster of healing," the "bench press of protection," the "barbell of deliverance," the "treadmill of safety." You have available to you the "leg press of soundness." All of these benefits were made available when you joined the club. How did you join? By making a decision to move from the position of slothfulness to the position of discipline and fitness.

When you got born again, you joined Club *Soteria,* and you now have available to you everything that's in the club. Deliverance is in the club. Safety is in the club. Healing and protection and soundness are in the club. Getting born again is the requirement for membership. But as soon as you become a member, you have a right to use everything that's in the club.

As an heir of salvation, I have a right to benefit from everything salvation has to offer. And one of those things is the ministry of angels. To continue the fitness club analogy, angels have been sent to act as personal trainers to the members of Club *Soteria*. Angels are employed at the club to assist you with those benefits of membership which have been made available to you.

Don't Neglect Your *Soteria*

Now, therefore, since we've become heirs of salvation, of *soteria,* and have the ministry of angels and all these other benefits of salvation available to us, the Bible says:

> **Therefore we ought to give the more earnest heed, to the things which we have heard** [from God's Word], **lest at any time we should let them slip.**
>
> **For if the word spoken by angels was stedfast, and every transgression and disobedience received a just recompence of reward; How shall we escape, if we neglect so great salvation...?**
>
> HEBREWS 2:1-3

How shall we escape trouble if we neglect our *soteria?* How shall we escape the report that we have cancer and are going to die next month? How shall we escape unemployment? How shall we escape depression? How shall we escape sin? How shall we escape poverty and lack? How shall we escape breakdown in our marriages? In short, how can we escape all the adverse circumstances we're faced with if we neglect so great *healing, deliverance, safety, soundness, protection* and the ministry of angels? How can we escape trouble if we don't take advantage of what was made available to us when we got born again?

Well, the answer is obvious, isn't it? I cannot escape if I neglect my *soteria*. But, praise the Lord, if I *don't* neglect my *soteria,* then *soteria* becomes my way of escape. My healing, my safety, my deliverance, my protection, my soundness, the ministry of angels—all that becomes my way of escape. If I'm going to benefit from my membership in Club *Soteria,* I have to pay attention to, and use what has been made available to me as a member. Otherwise, I won't be able to escape from the trouble I was in before I got born again. If I neglect my salvation, I won't be able to overcome trouble. I'll continue to live in defeat.

Pay Attention!

Why do people neglect their salvation? Of course one answer is they don't know about it. Why don't they know about it? They haven't read the Book. Why haven't they read the Book? Well, some of them are no doubt too lazy. But others have read it, or at least they've heard sermons about it; however, they still don't know who they are in Christ and what's available to them now that they're in that position. Why don't they know? *They don't pay attention!*

As a matter of fact, they don't *pay* at all. They don't pay the price that's necessary to benefit from what's available to them as members of Club *Soteria.* They're not willing to pay the fee, which in this case is *attention to the Word of God.* They don't exchange what they have for what God has.

You see, healing is available. Safety is available. Protection is available. Soundness is available. The ministry of angels is available but none of these things is of any benefit to you *until you pay for it.*

All the things included in *soteria* are available to the heirs of salvation, but the heirs have not been willing to pay for them.

And what do we have to pay? What is the medium of exchange? *Attention.* The Bible says:

> **Attend to my words; incline thine ear unto my sayings.**
>
> **Let thine eyes look right on, and let thine eyelids look straight before thee.... Turn not to the right hand nor to the left....**
>
> **PROVERBS 4:20,25,27**

What you attend to is what you will become. Desires are created by what you attend to.

Whatever measure of attention a person pays to something, that's the amount of that something he will receive in his life. Why? Because the Bible says you will reap what you sow (Galatians 6:7). And with whatever measure you measure out, it will be measured back to you (Luke 6:38).

Therefore, if I pay more attention to the things of darkness than I do to the things of light, what kind of mentality have I created in myself? A darkness mentality. And I'll have it because I paid for it. I paid for darkness and therefore, I received darkness. I will reap what I sowed by *paying attention* to the things of the kingdom of darkness. The medium of exchange, the coin or the currency I used to purchase a darkness mentality, was *attention.* I've now paid for the trouble in my life by paying attention to the words of the devil. But if I pay attention to the Word of God, I will receive all the benefits of salvation that are promised to me as an heir of salvation.

You see, all we have to do to receive the benefits of our membership in Club *Soteria* is give heed or pay attention to the things which we have heard from the Word of God. And we must be careful not to neglect those benefits or let them slip out of our consciousness.

This **so great salvation** is available to us because Jesus paid the price for it. We don't have to buy it because Jesus has already bought it with His blood. With His blood He purchased healing. With His blood He purchased soundness. With His blood He purchased deliverance and protection and safety. The equipment I need to use has already been purchased by the management of the club. All I need to do is join the club and start exercising my rights and privileges as a member.

And we must be careful not to do what so many members do when they join a club. They pay the price or the fee, sign the contract, get their name on the membership list, make a commitment to a workout program and then they never show up for training. They never show up. All the equipment that has been made available to club members is there waiting for them. They have a right to use it; they paid the price to use it; they've made the commitment to use it. They said with their mouth they're going to use it. They've signed a document declaring that they've made a commitment to use the equipment and get in shape. But they never show up to use it. That's why the Bible says:

> **Be not slothful, but followers of them who through faith and patience inherit the promises** [of God].

> **HEBREWS 6:12**

Every person who has been born again is a member of Club *Soteria*. All the benefits that are included in salvation are available to every member, but too few members are using those benefits. They haven't paid sufficient attention to what's available to them. They neglect to use their salvation because they haven't attended to the Word of God enough to know what the benefits of their salvation really are.

Club Member's Benefit Package

The benefits of salvation or *soteria* are described in Psalm 103. Like the writer of Hebrews, the psalmist tells us not to forget or neglect the benefits of our membership in Club *Soteria:*

Bless the Lord, O my soul, and forget not all his benefits:

Who forgiveth all thine iniquities; who healeth all they diseases;

Who redeemeth thy life from destruction; who crowneth thee with lovingkindness and tender mercies;

Who satisfieth thy mouth with good things; so that thy youth is renewed like the eagle's.

The Lord executeth righteousness and judgment for all that are oppressed.

PSALM 103:2-6

Benefit No. 1: Forgiveness

The first benefit of salvation is forgiveness, not just for some of our sins but for all of them. **Who forgiveth *all* thine iniquities** (v. 3). As a member of Club *Soteria,* I receive forgiveness for all my iniquities. Before I got born again and became a member of the club, I walked around piling sin on top of sin, and I didn't have any detergent with which to wash them off. The best I could do was cover my sins and hide them from sight temporarily. In the Old Testament, the blood sacrifices of bulls and goats didn't take away sins; they just covered them up for a year (Hebrews 10:1-4). But with His blood Jesus bought deliverance from sin once and for all

(Hebrews 10:10). And now because I am an heir of salvation and a member of Club *Soteria,* my transgressions have been removed from me **as far as the east is from the west** (Psalm 103:12).

Benefit No. 2: Healing

The second benefit of membership in Club *Soteria* is healing. The Lord **healeth all thy diseases** (Psalm 103:3). As an heir of salvation, I don't have to automatically accept the bad report when I go to the doctor, and the doctor tells me I have an incurable disease. It may be true that outside of Club *Soteria,* for people who are not members, there is no cure for that disease. But I'm a member of the club. Healing is a benefit I have a right to receive as a member. And therefore, when sickness and disease show up to trouble me, I recall to mind the benefits of my **so great salvation** and say to my angels, "Ministering spirits, healing belongs to me. Go forth and bring my healing to me in accordance with the Word of God which says He **healeth all thy diseases.**"

Benefit No. 3: Redeemed from Destruction

Thirdly, my life is redeemed from destruction as a result of my membership in Club *Soteria.* In these days of danger and violence, that's a benefit I can't afford to neglect. Because I am an heir of salvation, my life has been redeemed from airplane crashes and from car crashes. My life has been redeemed from stray bullets. My life has been redeemed from contagious diseases. My life has been redeemed from rape, from muggings, from robbery and murder and kidnapping. My life has been redeemed from natural disasters. Protection is one of the benefits included in *soteria.* And as long as

I don't forget about it, as long as I don't neglect it, I have the right to claim it any time I'm threatened with any type of destruction. Instead of being fearful and troubled, I just need to recall to mind that the ministry of angels is available to me.

> **For he shall give his angels charge over thee, to keep thee in all thy ways.**

> **They shall bear thee up in their hands, lest thou dash thy foot against a stone.**

> PSALM 91:11,12

Whenever I'm in danger, I just need to recall that according to the Word of God, angels are waiting to carry me to safety.

Benefit No. 4: Lovingkindness and Tender Mercy

As a member of Club *Soteria,* I also wear the crown of God's lovingkindness and tender mercies (Psalm 103:4). As a member of the club, I receive things I don't deserve, things I haven't even asked for and that I didn't even know I could have. Because I am an heir of salvation, God's mercy outlasts my sin. I have access to His grace, to undeserved favor, to His lovingkindness. Child of God, no one can be kind the way God can be kind. No one can show tenderness and mercy the way God can show tenderness and mercy. God is love, and His lovingkindness and tender mercies are available to me even when I'm at my most unlovable.

Benefit No. 5: My Youth Is Renewed Like the Eagle's

The fifth benefit of salvation is described in verse 5 of Psalm 103:

Who satisfieth thy mouth with good things; so that thy youth is renewed like the eagle's.

God satisfies us with good things for a reason so our youth can be renewed like an eagle's. The renewal of your youth is based on how you choose to use those good things that God has satisfied your mouth with. Words come from your mouth, and if you go around talking about how old you're getting, you'll talk yourself right into a river of wrinkles. Don't do that. Let the Word of God satisfy your mouth. Let the Word of God come out of your mouth, and each birthday say, "Hallelujah, my youth is renewed like the eagle's! I'm getting older and better, praise God. I'm like fine wine. The longer I sit the better I get!"

Benefit No. 6: Escape From Oppression

And finally, the sixth benefit of salvation is escape from oppression.

The Lord executeth righteousness and judgment for all that are oppressed.

PSALM 103:6

If you're being troubled by depression and your spirit is being oppressed, you need to pay special attention to this benefit of salvation. These days we can't escape oppression if we neglect our salvation and forget our benefits. But if we are diligent to attend to God's Word and claim by faith the benefits of our membership in Club *Soteria,* God will free us from all our oppressions and depressions.

Just the First Step

Getting born again, joining Club *Soteria,* and learning what our benefits are as members is not all there is to learning to trouble our trouble. But learning who we are in Christ, and paying attention to what the Word of God says is available to us as heirs of salvation, is an essential first step.

If we're to overcome trouble in our lives and live in the victory Jesus bought for us at Calvary, we have to put down roots deep in the Word of God so we never forget the benefits of our *soteria*.

I'll talk more about getting rooted in the Word in the next chapter. But you don't have to wait until you've read any farther in this book to begin recalling the benefits of your salvation and putting those benefits to work in your life. Get in the habit of confessing God's Word. To make sure you aren't neglecting a single benefit you're entitled to, say the following confession out loud daily:

In the Name of Jesus, I am learning how to trouble trouble. I am not of this world system. I live in this world, but I am not of this world. I am of the household of faith. I am of the Word, and in the Word I'll have peace and security in the midst of trouble.

In the world I'll have tribulation, but in the Word, I'll have peace. Therefore, I'm in this world but living in the Word, so I'm going to be of good cheer because Jesus has overcome the world. And this is the victory that overcomes the world even our faith.

I declare right now that I'm an heir of salvation. I'm an heir of *soteria*.

Angels hearken unto the words that I speak from God's Word. They have been sent to minister to me, to serve me.

Therefore, I will hearken and take earnest heed to the things that I have heard and not let them slip. And I will escape because I will pay due attention to my *soteria,* my deliverance, my healing, my soundness, my safety, my protection, and the ministry of angels. I will give the necessary attention to get what has been made available to me.

And in the Name of Jesus, I declare my benefits. Just as a lawyer reading a will declares how each heir benefits from what has been left behind, I declare my benefits. He forgives me of all my iniquities. He heals all of my diseases. He redeems my life from destruction. He crowns my head with lovingkindness and tender mercies. He renews my youth as the eagle's and fills my mouth with good things that satisfy me. With long life shall He satisfy me and show me my salvation. He executes righteousness and judgment for all who are oppressed.

I am an heir of *soteria*. Jesus has paid the price and now I make the choice to join the club.

I choose life. And in Jesus' name, from this moment on, starting today, I am going to trouble trouble. When trouble is in my way, I'll move it.

Trouble will come but it will no longer overcome me. It will no longer overcome my life, my finances, my peace, my relationships, my position.

I am rooted in the Word of God, and my house is built on a rock. I will not be moved, ever! In Jesus' name. Amen.

---

[1] James Strong, "A Greek Dictionary of the New Testament", *Strong's Exhaustive Concordance of the Bible,* (Nashville: Abingdon, 1890), p. 70, #4991.

2

STAY IN THE WATER

Developing Roots in the Word of God

By now some of you may be saying, "Brother Dollar, I've been meditating on the benefits of my membership in Club *Soteria*. I've been attending to the Word of God and confessing it out loud like you taught us in the last chapter, but now I'm seeing more trouble in my life than I ever saw before. I hear what you're saying about overcoming trouble, but it sure looks like things in my life are getting worse instead of better! What's happening here?"

Well, what's happening is exactly what Jesus said would happen. Remember, He said in John 16:33:

In the world ye shall have tribulation.

Now, as I said in the introduction to this section, when Jesus speaks of "the world," He is referring to the world's system of values and the world's way of doing things. And He says that as long as you are living in the world, in the world system, you are going to have trouble. Don't be surprised when trouble shows up, because according to Jesus, as long as you are in the world — and particularly as long as you are operating according to the world's system — trouble is going to come.

But Jesus also says in that same verse:

These things I have spoken unto you, that in me ye might have peace.

JOHN 16:33

Now what is He speaking? He's speaking words. He says in effect, "The words I have spoken unto you have given you peace." So I submit to you right now that *peace comes from hearing the words that Jesus has spoken.* Peace comes from the Word of God, from the *Word system,* from God's way of doing things. Jesus makes it clear in John 16:33 that in the world system, you're going to have tribulation. But in the Word system, you're going to have peace.

Therefore, you have to choose which system to operate in while you are living in this world. As born again believers, we are *in* this world, but we are not *of* this world. We live physically in this natural world, but we don't operate according to the system of this world. We operate according to the system of the Word of God which produces peace.

See to It

But if, according to Jesus, we are going to have tribulation and trouble as long as we live in the world, how are we supposed to deal with trouble? How are we going to have peace when there is all this trouble coming against us? What did Jesus mean when He said, **Be of good cheer; I have overcome the world** (John 16:33)? That seems like a strange thing to say, doesn't it? Right in the middle of telling us we're going to have trouble, He says to be of good cheer — or as we might say, be joyful or "get happy" — because **I have overcome the world.** What's the significance of Jesus having overcome the world? Well, *if Jesus has overcome the world, He has given us, His children, everything we need to overcome the world.*

Jesus expects us to learn how to overcome trouble. In Matthew 24, He tells us that even in the midst of the worst kind of trouble, we are to see to it that we are not troubled.

> **Take heed that no man deceive you. For many shall come in my name, saying, I am Christ; and shall deceive many. And ye shall hear of wars and rumours of wars: see that ye be not troubled: for all these things must come to pass, but the end is not yet.**
>
> MATTHEW 24:4-6

Now, if you have your Bible and a pen handy, I want you to underline the phrase *see that ye be not troubled*. That's an important point because here again, just as He did in John 16:33, Jesus said trouble is going to come, but we are not to allow it to trouble us. However, it would not be right for God to say to us **see that ye be not troubled,** but not to provide us the means to see to it we are not troubled. Therefore, since He said it, there obviously must be something available to us that we can use to see that we are not troubled. If someone tells me to see that I'm not troubled without showing me what I need to do and what I can do to see that I'm not troubled, then in all likelihood, I'm going to wind up in trouble. If I'm responsible for seeing to it that I'm not troubled, I've got to know what action to take to overcome trouble.

A Different Perspective

The requirement that I see that I'm not troubled gives me a different perspective on the subject of troubling my trouble. You see, it is now not the devil who's responsible for my being troubled. I am now the one who is responsible for whether I'm troubled or not. In John 14:1 Jesus said, **Let not your heart be troubled.** The implication is that if I can *let not* my heart be troubled, I can also *let* my heart be troubled. So it is up to me whether I'm going to allow myself to be troubled or whether I'm going to trouble my trouble. Obviously, there is something I do to be troubled, and there is something I do to not be troubled.

So it's now my decision whether I'm troubled or not. Jesus is saying that I have authority over trouble. If I don't want to be troubled, I don't have to be troubled. It doesn't matter how much trouble is around me. I don't have to let it overcome me because I have the authority given me by the Word of God and by my position as a member of Club *Soteria* to overcome trouble.

But as we've seen already, it takes a lot more to overcome trouble in our lives than just knowing mentally that we have authority over trouble. It takes more than knowing the benefits of our salvation and confessing those benefits out loud a few times to put trouble to flight. God has provided every weapon we need to overcome trouble, but until we get firmly established in the Word of God, we won't be successful in using those weapons. In order to learn how to use our weapons to trouble trouble, it is necessary first of all to put down roots in the Word. And putting down roots in the Word is very important. As you're learning to trouble your trouble, the devil will be fighting every step of the way to steal the Word out of your heart.

Its Own Roots

Years ago, when my mother would go to visit a friend's house, she would often see a houseplant she liked. If she didn't have that particular species of plant, she would ask her friend if she could break a little piece of the plant off and take it home. I used to watch her do that, and I'd wonder, *what is she up to?* Instead of going to the nursery and buying a whole plant, she'd say, "Just let me have a little piece of this plant." Then, when she got home, she'd stick that little piece of plant in a jar of water, and the plant would just stay in that water, day in and day out.

Day in and day out, day after day after day, that little piece of plant sat in that water. I'd look at it just sitting there, not looking like it was doing anything, and I'd think, *what's going on here?* You would think if you broke a piece of plant off its life source — that is, off the main plant — it would wither up and die. I'd look at that little piece of plant my mother broke off the main plant and stuck in water, and I'd see it sitting there in the water day after day, month after month. I'd think, *that thing is never going to grow.*

But then, one day, I'd walk through the room where that little piece of plant was sitting in the same jar of water it had been in for months. And I'd see that little piece of plant had developed its own roots. It didn't have to depend on the roots of the original plant anymore. It had stayed in the water long enough to develop its own roots. It could be planted in soil because, now it had the ability to draw nourishment directly from its life source.

Satan's Objective

What Satan wants to do the minute he sees you're beginning to get a revelation from the Word of God about your rights and benefits as a born again believer, is to come immediately and steal that Word out of your heart. He wants to steal the Word before you have time to develop any roots. He wants to break you off from your life source and keep you away from it long enough for you to wither up and die. But what God wants you to do is stay in the water — the water of the Word (Ephesians 5:26) — long enough to develop roots of your own. Because you're not going to produce fruit until you have roots. So if the devil can steal the Word from you before it develops a root in you and you become established in it, you'll never get the fruit the Word is supposed to produce in your life.

The key to developing the root of what you get from God's Word is to stay *in the water* day in and day out, just like that little piece of plant of my mother's, until you finally develop a root. And once you get the root, you're guaranteed the fruit. You can eat fruit off the Word once you're rooted in it. However, the devil knows if you develop roots in God's Word you're going to be able to overcome all the trouble he's throwing at you. So his first objective is to keep you out of the Word.

The Bible says we shouldn't be surprised if trouble seems to increase the minute we start applying the Word to our lives. Paul says:

> **...all that will live godly in Christ** [the Anointed] **Jesus shall suffer persecution.**

> **2 TIMOTHY 3:12**

And Peter warns us:

> **Beloved, think it not strange concerning the fiery trial which is to try you, as though some strange thing happened unto you.**

> **1 PETER 4:12**

Unfortunately, there seem to be many faith people who think it's a strange thing if they have some persecution. They seem to have the idea that because they now walk by faith, they're not supposed to have problems.

But of course that's not true. The Bible tells us to expect persecution and trouble to increase when we get born again, because the devil is desperate to keep the Word of God from taking root and producing fruit in our lives. In Mark 4, Jesus explained Satan's part in our trouble in the parable of the sower.

The Enemy's Part

In Mark 4:14 Jesus says:

The sower soweth the word.

So right now, as you're reading this book, I am sowing the Word. I am planting the Word. And you are attending to the Word and not letting it depart from your eyes (Proverbs 4:21). And the Word is going through your eye-gate into your heart.

Jesus continues in verse 15:

And these are they by the way side, where the word is sown; but when they have heard, Satan cometh...

Satan comes when? Tomorrow? Next month? In two hours and a half? No!

Satan cometh *immediately* and taketh away the word that was sown in their hearts.

MARK 4:15

Now notice that Satan shows up for a very specific reason — to get the Word. So that answers the question of why you are having more trouble and tribulation now, than you had before you got born again, or when you were in a church that didn't give you the Word. Now that you're born again, now that you're reading a book about how to apply the Word to your life and get results, Satan knows the fruit that can be produced from the Word if it develops a root in you. Therefore, he comes *immediately* because he knows that if he can get there as soon as possible, he can take from you what you've received before it has time to develop a root.

If Satan can steal the Word from you before it develops a root, you'll have no chance of bearing fruit and giving him problems. So right now, as you're reading this page, Satan is outside plotting. He is planning ways to take the Word you're receiving before you've had time to stay in it long enough to get rooted and established in it.

Jesus goes on to point out the dangers of having no roots.

And these are they likewise which are sown on stony ground; who, when they have heard the word, immediately receive it with gladness; And have no root in themselves, and so endure but for a time...

MARK 4:16,17

Why do they have no root? They didn't stay in the water long enough. They immediately heard the Word with gladness, but they didn't hold on to it. You see, you may be thrilled and excited when you first get a revelation from God's Word. But if, when your emotions cool off, you allow the devil to come in and steal the Word, you will never benefit from the fruit you could have produced from that Word once it had developed a root. And the only way you're going to develop roots in God's Word is to spend time in that Word just as that little piece of plant spends time in the jar of water. It stays in the water until it develops its own root, giving it the ability to produce its own fruit.

Jesus now tells us why persecutions and afflictions come.

...When affliction or persecution ariseth for the word's sake...

MARK 4:17

So we know afflictions and persecutions arise for the Word's sake.

...immediately they are offended.

MARK 4:17

If you don't have enough root to keep you "strapped down" in the position of gladness you were in when you first heard the Word, you'll get upset and offended. When you're persecuted and afflicted or troubled because you're trying to live by God's Word, pretty soon you'll begin to neglect your *soteria* and let the things you have heard slip out of your consciousness. When that happens, you won't overcome trouble — trouble will overcome you.

Choking the Word

If the devil can't steal the Word out of your heart immediately, and he can't make you let go of it through persecution and afflictions, he still has three more weapons he can try to use on you.

> **And these are they which are sown among thorns; such as hear the word, And *the cares of this world,* and *the deceitfulness of riches,* and *the lusts of other things* entering in, choke the word, and it becometh unfruitful.**

MARK 4:18,19

The cares of this world come from looking at television news all day long. They come from reading all the daily newspapers, seeing all the problems in the world, and listening to all of the bad reports. What happens when you pay attention to the cares of this world? The cares of this world become larger in your mind than the Word of God. When there's not a sufficiency of God's Word in you, not enough roots to hold out against all this "stuff" you're taking in from the world, the cares of the world outweigh the Word of God.

Then they choke, block up and stop the Word from bearing fruit and bringing results in your life.

The Word can also be choked by **the deceitfulness of riches** and **the lusts of other things.** Riches are deceitful because they give the impression that they can provide all your needs. God doesn't mind you having riches, but He doesn't want you to be deceived into thinking money can do everything. Money can buy a lot of things, but it can't buy everything. Jesus said it's very difficult for someone who trusts in riches to enter into the kingdom of God (Mark 10:24). So if you expect money to keep you from having trouble, you're being deceived.

The Word can also be choked and made unfruitful in your life if you let **the lusts of other things** take up all your time and attention. Remember, I said we must not neglect to pay attention to the Word of God. Whatever gets most of your attention and time will become the biggest part of your life. Unless you spend more time in the Word than you do with other things, it will not develop roots and bear fruit in your life. And it's the devil's objective to choke the Word out of your life so that you don't get any results from it.

The Process of Receiving the Word

We see that Satan's objective is to keep us from bearing fruit, or to keep the Word from bearing fruit in our lives. Jesus said those **such as hear the word, and receive it** will **bring forth fruit** (Mark 4:20). However, since the people He describes in verses 15-19 also heard the Word but didn't produce fruit, obviously something has to happen between hearing the Word and bringing forth fruit.

Jesus said we have to *receive* the Word. Now what does "receiving the Word" mean? It means going through the process of developing roots. It means going through the process of growing roots in the Word.

So now we come to my part in the process of overcoming *my* trouble. I can't just hear the Word preached or read it and then go about my business. I must stay with that Word. I must stay in the water until I develop a root. The Word has not been properly received unless a root has developed. The ground cannot properly receive a plant if the plant doesn't have any roots. So the Word cannot produce fruit in me unless I let it develop roots. The root is the life of a plant. And the Word of God has to produce life in me before I can bring forth any fruit from it in this natural world.

You've Got to Live With It

How do I give life to the Word which I have heard? Just stay in the Word until the roots start growing. I don't know how long it will be before the roots develop. I never could tell how long it would be before those little pieces of plant my mother put in the jars of water would develop roots. It didn't look like anything was happening for months and months. Then all of a sudden, one day little roots would be floating around in the water.

It's the same way with the Word of God. You have to stay in the Word until the roots grow. Just let the water of God's Word continue to remain in your life. Then one day, you'll look up and see you have a root and that you have the life of God in you. Now you're ready to plant it and receive the fruit of it.

Do you see where you may have been missing it? You can't just hear a sermon or read a certain passage of Scripture and say, "Well, glory to God, I've got that" — and then go out and forget it in the next two days. You have to live with that Scripture. You have to live with it. You have to stay with that Word until it develops roots and the fruit comes.

Instead of trying to read a different Scripture every day, take the area of your life that needs work. If it's your health that needs work, get all the Scriptures on healing and live with them until the fruit of healing is produced. If you have financial problems, stay with Scriptures on prosperity and provision until they bear fruit in your finances. If you need deliverance, get the Word of God on deliverance. Read those Scriptures over every day. Confess them out loud. Study them. Listen to tapes that teach on them.

"Well, Brother Dollar, how long do I keep that up?"

Until it starts bearing fruit. Don't quit until you get results. Just stay in the water of the Word until you're healed and prosperous and delivered. The key to breakthrough is consistency. You have to stay with the Word until it begins to consistently bear fruit in your life.

Get a piece of the Word that speaks to the area of your need, put it in the water, and then stay there. For months or even years if you have to. Just stay with it. Stay with it until it produces.

What I Have to Do

Now, how is it that I let not my heart be troubled? How is it that I see that I be not troubled? What is it that I do to make sure that trouble doesn't overcome me? What do *I* have to do? What is my part — not the devil's part, not God's part, but my part in troubling my trouble? The answer is in Psalm 112.

> **Praise ye the Lord. Blessed is the man that feareth the Lord, that delighteth greatly in his commandments.**

His seed shall be mighty upon earth: the generation of the upright shall be blessed.

Wealth and riches shall be in his house: and his righteousness endureth for ever.

Unto the upright there ariseth light in the darkness: he is gracious, and full of compassion, and righteous.

A good man sheweth favour, and lendeth: he will guide his affairs with discretion.

Surely he shall not be moved for ever: the righteous shall be in everlasting remembrance.

He shall not be afraid of evil tidings: his heart is fixed, trusting in the Lord.

PSALM 112:1-7

Now I want to know: how did this man get himself established in a place where he could not be moved forever? How did he get to a place where he is not afraid of evil tidings, where he is not afraid of afflictions or of persecutions or of trouble? The Bible says he is in that place because his heart is fixed.

What is his heart fixed on?

The Word of God. A heart that is fixed on God's Word and trusts in the Lord will not be troubled, no matter what happens.

How Do You Get It?

How do you get a fixed or established heart?

Stay in the Word. Stay in the water. If you're having trouble trusting God in some area, fix your heart on what the Word of God says about that.

For example, I used to have trouble trusting God for finances. I had a problem giving tithes and offerings because it always seemed to me that I needed my money a whole lot more than God needed it. Since the Bible says God owns the cattle on a thousand hills (Psalm 50:10), I wondered why He needed my little 10 percent. I didn't have any trust in what I heard preached from the Word about giving and receiving.

But I knew that my inability to trust God to get my financial needs met was my problem, not His. Fortunately, I'd been taught to go to the Word to get help to solve a problem, so that's what I did. I said, "Let's get in the Word and see what it says about trusting God for finances, about tithing and giving offerings, about giving and receiving." So I flooded my mind and my heart with what the Word says about those areas where I was having trouble trusting God.

And the more Word that came into my heart, and the longer I stayed in the water, the more roots I developed. I became more established until now I can trust God for finances.

At first, I could not trust Him because my heart was not fixed. But now that my heart is fixed and established on God's Word about finances, I can see that I am not troubled when the devil attacks my finances, or when there is some lack or financial need in my life. I don't have to be afraid of some bad report, some "evil tidings," about the stock market or the economy or unemployment because having my heart fixed on God's Word defeats fear. I am not **afraid of evil tidings** because my **heart is fixed, trusting in the Lord** (Psalm 112:7).

Child of God, the only way to trouble your trouble is with the Word of God. And you can't use the Word as a weapon to overcome trouble until you become rooted and grounded in it. But before you can become rooted in something, you have to develop roots. And developing roots requires staying in the water of the Word long enough to become fixed and established in it. Get in the Word and stay in it until the answer comes. Stay with the Scriptures that speak to your need until you get results. Be patient, be consistent. The Bible promises that if you will stay in the Word, victory will come.

> **This book of the law** [the Word of God] **shall not depart out of thy mouth; but thou shalt meditate therein day and night, that thou mayest observe to do according to all that is written therein: for then thou shalt make thy way prosperous, and then thou shalt have good success.**
>
> JOSHUA 1:8

In the next four chapters of this book, I'm going to be showing you how to use specific areas of Scripture as weapons to trouble your trouble. Don't be surprised if, as you first begin learning these scriptural weapons and getting rooted and established in them, you seem to be having more trouble than ever. Remember, the devil is out to steal the Word from you. But if you are consistent and patient about staying in the water until you grow roots in the Word and get your heart fixed on it, your victory will come. Then once you develop roots, you will bear fruit.

While you're in the process of staying in the water and developing roots, pray the following prayer daily:

Father, in the name of Jesus, Jesus said that He has given me peace through what He has said. He said that in this world I will have tribulation, but that I should be of good cheer because He has overcome the world.

If Jesus has overcome the world, then I can overcome the world because the Bible says this is the victory that overcomes the world, even my faith.

Thank you, Lord, I overcome the world with my faith.

And, Father, I thank You in the name of Jesus that they that live godly shall outlast persecution. I am outlasting all persecution today no matter what is coming to me. I will outlast it today, and I will come out with great victory. Thank You, Lord, my heart is being fixed on that right now.

I am trusting You, Father, that I'm overcoming trouble right now, and I am establishing in my heart that just because trouble comes, it doesn't have to overcome. I'm establishing my heart that I'm the overcomer of trouble, and trouble is not the overcomer of me.

I trust You, Lord, and I'm delighting in Your commandments, and therefore, wealth and riches shall be in my house. I am planting the seed of the Word of God in my heart, and I thank You, Lord, that I will not be moved forever. In the name of Jesus. Amen.

3

TROUBLING YOUR TROUBLE
WITH THE FORCE OF PEACE

Part 1: Peace From the Word

The first weapon from God's Word we will learn to use to trouble our trouble is the force of peace. In the previous chapter we learned that peace comes from hearing the words Jesus has spoken. Jesus said in John 16:33:

> **These things I have spoken unto you, that in me ye might have peace.**

Therefore, since I have heard the words Jesus has spoken, I must have peace already. Right in the midst of all this trouble, Jesus says I have peace.

Well, if I have peace, what do I have it for? If God has given me peace, He must have given it to me for a reason. He must have had a purpose. And I need to find out what that purpose is because if you don't know the purpose for a thing, abuse is inevitable.

So if I have peace, I need to find out "what for?" What is peace? Where does it come from? How do I use it? And how will it benefit me? Particularly, how will it benefit me here in the world system where I'm in the midst of all this trouble and tribulation?

Pursue It

Peace is *security in the midst of turmoil.* But there's a lot more to the force of peace than just calm in the middle of a storm. The Bible places such a high value on peace that it says we should actively **seek peace and pursue it** (Psalm 34:14). *The Amplified Bible* tells us in that same verse to **seek, inquire for, and crave peace and pursue (go after) it!** So finding peace is an action on my part. I go after peace. I pursue it. I crave it — I am thirsty, hungry, desperate for it. I am continually looking for it.

And then when I find peace, the Bible says I am to *live in peace.* Peace is to be a way of life.

> **Finally, brethren...***live in peace,* **and [then] the God of love [Who is the Source of affection, goodwill, love, and benevolence toward men] and the Author and Promoter of peace will be with you.**
>
> 2 CORINTHIANS **13:11,** AMP

According to the Word of God, living in peace is the way all born-again believers should live.

A Spiritual Force

Peace is listed in Galatians 5:22 and 23 as a component of the fruit of the Spirit.

> **But the fruit of the Spirit is love, joy, peace, longsuffering, gentleness, goodness, faith,**
>
> **Meekness, temperance: against such there is no law.**

The fruit of the Spirit are forces of every believer's recreated spirit. Therefore, since peace is a fruit of the Spirit, peace is a force.

Every believer gets the seed of peace when he gets born again. Now that you're born again, peace is a force that's abiding on the inside of your recreated spirit. And the Bible says that against peace there is no law.

Now what does that mean? In Romans 8:2, Paul tells us about two opposing laws: the law of the Spirit of life in Christ Jesus and the law of sin and death. And he says:

> **The law of the Spirit of life in Christ Jesus hath made me free from the law of sin and death.**

> **ROMANS 8:2**

You see, trouble operates under the law of sin and death. But peace operates under the law of life which is in Christ Jesus. And **against such there is no law** (Galatians 5:23). In other words, Paul says, when you operate in this peace, there is no law in the world system that can stop peace from doing what God promised it will do.

Once you claim the benefits of your salvation and start operating in peace, there is no trouble which can trouble your peace. There is no law in the world system, no law of sin and death, that can stop peace from producing what God intended for it to produce. Trouble can't stop peace. Why? Because trouble is under the law of sin and death, but peace is under the law of the Spirit of life in Christ Jesus. And since the law of the Spirit of life in Christ Jesus has made you free from the law of sin and death, trouble can't stop peace from producing in your life what God created it to produce.

Hallelujah! That's good news! Peace has made me free from trouble. Trouble may come, but I don't have to be locked up and tangled up in bondage to it. I can be free from trouble because I'm in peace, and there is no law in this physical world that can stop the peace of God. It doesn't matter how bad the trouble is. Once you have peace, you are in security because peace cannot be stopped.

What Is Peace?

Let's look a little deeper now into the definition of peace. First of all, peace is *a state of rest*. You know when you rest from something, you cease from labor. You're not trying to make something happen. You're resting in what has already happened. You're in a state of rest, in a state of having ceased from labor.

Secondly, as we've already said, peace is *security in the midst of turmoil*. But if peace is security, what creates that security? Now I know you're going to say, "the Word of God," but why is the Word of God my security? Suppose I've just gotten born again and don't know anything about the Bible. What am I supposed to understand when you tell me the Word of God is my security in the midst of trouble? Why is the Word of God secure?

"It works," you say. But I don't know it works. You do because you've had experience with it, but I haven't had any experience yet. There's something I have to know before I can have peace.

You see, if I'm a new believer, you can't just blurt out a bunch of "religious" answers and expect those answers to give me peace. I'm going to look at all the trouble you're going through and ask you, "How did you get peace in the midst of that just by reading what God said?"

Obviously something happened to you when you read the Word, but you can't just tell me to read the Word and expect me to automatically have peace and security. I've got bills that need to be paid.

"Oh," you say, "the Lord will work it out."

But how do you expect me to have peace that the Lord will work it out when the landlord is coming to evict me from my house tomorrow? What's my security in this situation? Tell me why I ought to be secure in God's Word.

"Well," you say, "God says His Word will not return to Him void, but it will accomplish everything it was sent to accomplish" (Isaiah 55:11). How do I know that?

"Have faith."

But how do I know that having faith in the Word is really going to work for me? What's my guarantee?

The Guarantee

By now I know you may be getting upset with me for asking all these questions and then objecting to your answers, but if you'll bear with me a minute, I'll explain. I'm trying to get you to see a very important point.

Let's use a simple example. If you told me that you were going to do something for me — for instance, that you were going to pay my rent — why should I have security that you're really going to do it? Can I depend on you to do what you promised *just because you said it?* If I didn't know you very well, I might hesitate to depend on your word. But suppose you brought me a written contract, drawn up by a legal expert, properly signed and witnessed — then I would believe you. I can depend on what that contract says because the contract is *suable.* If you don't do what the contract says you will do, I can take you to court under the clauses of the contract, and make you perform the promised work or pay damages to compensate me. The contract you signed is my security because it's a legal *covenant.*

That's what the Bible is. It's a covenant. In Genesis 15, God cut a covenant with Abraham. He walked in the blood between the two halves of the animals He told Abraham to cut up (Genesis 15:17), and He swore an oath — the book of Hebrews says He swore by Himself since there wasn't anyone greater to swear by (Hebrews 6:13). God made a promise in blood. He cut a covenant with Abraham and his seed (Genesis 15:18).

Now who is Abraham's seed? I am and you are.

...If ye be Christ's, then are ye Abraham's seed, and heirs according to the promise.

GALATIANS 3:29

God, willing more abundantly to shew unto the heirs of promise the immutability [unchangeability] **of his counsel, confirmed it by an oath:**

That by two immutable things, in which it was impossible for God to lie, we might have a strong consolation....

HEBREWS 6:17,18

God's Word is a sworn covenant between Himself and all of us who believe Jesus is the Christ. It's an oath and a promise sworn in two unchangeable things — the body and blood of Jesus Christ. God's Word is good because He is unchangeable, and He can't lie. The question is not whether God will do what He said just because He said it. The question is, how can He not do it because of His sacrifice of Jesus, and the fact that He said it in blood? God cannot lie. Since God is holding up the universe by the power of His Word (Hebrews 1:3), if He broke His Word, heaven and earth would pass away. The terms of a blood covenant state that *if you don't keep your bargain, if you don't keep your word, you have to die.*

So if God didn't keep His Word, He'd have to die. And of course, since there is no death in God, He's not going to die. God can't lie, and therefore, if He said He would do something, He has to do it. If He spoke it,

He will bring it to pass. And glory to God, that's my guarantee. That's my security. I am secure in the blood covenant of God Almighty in which He swore that what He said He will surely bring to pass.

That's how I can have faith. Because I have a covenant. That's how I can believe God's Word. Because I have a covenant, a covenant sworn in blood. And that's why I can have peace — because I have a covenant of peace (Isaiah 54:10). I'm guaranteed security in the midst of turmoil because God swore an oath in blood to give it to me.

"World" Peace Versus "Word" Peace

We can have security in God's Word because He swore an oath. He signed His name to a contract. Jesus said that His words were spoken to bring us peace.

> **If a man love me, he will keep my words.... He that loveth me not keepeth not my sayings: and the word which ye hear is not mine, but the Father's which sent me. These things have I spoken unto you, being yet present with you. But the Comforter, which is the Holy Ghost, whom the Father will send in my name, he shall teach you all things, and bring all things to your remembrance, whatsoever I have said unto**

you. Peace I leave with you, my peace I give unto you: not as the world giveth, give I unto you. Let not your heart be troubled, neither let it be afraid.

JOHN 14:23-27

Let's pay attention to the progression here. The Father spoke words one day. Jesus came and spoke the same words the Father spoke. The Holy Ghost is on His way, and He will speak the same thing that Jesus spoke. So the words that Jesus spoke, which are recorded in the New Testament, are the words of the Father.

Now in verse 27, Jesus said, **Peace I leave with you,** *my peace I give unto you: not as the world giveth....* There is a great difference between the peace of the Lord and the peace of the world.

Many of you no doubt remember that before you got born again, you experienced a certain kind of peace. There is a kind of peace that the world can give. You experienced peace when you graduated from high school or college, when you got that job, when you got that raise, when you got a good report from the doctor — when everything in your life was going well, you had peace.

But notice what your peace was based on. Your peace was based on worldly systems and circumstances. And the trouble was, once the world systems started falling apart and failing, your peace fell apart and failed with them. When you lost your job, your peace went with it. When you lost your salary, your peace went with it. When you found out the boss didn't like you anymore because you didn't show up at the office cocktail party, your peace was destroyed.

It's impossible to depend on the world for peace because the world is changing all the time. People in the world are double-minded and unstable in all their ways. One day they're up; the next day they're down. One day they praise this and praise that, and the next day they curse the very same things. The world is up and down, up and down all the time. You cannot invest your peace in it because it is always subject to change.

But Jesus said He gave us *His peace.* And the peace that comes from God always outweighs the peace that comes from the world because God never changes. When you get into God's system, when you join Club *Soteria* by getting born again, you're not subject to what the world does. When you're in God, you are rich whether there's a recession or not because God's Word says you are (2 Corinthians 8:9), and God can't lie. But if you're depending on the world system, when the world economy crashes, your economy has to crash along with it.

No Security in the World

I thought I had security when I was in the world system. I thought I knew how the world system worked and how to work it. All I had to do, I thought, was to go to school, get a degree, get a job, make plenty of money and then I would be happy. Not true, I found out! Because there was one thing I was missing with my degree and my job and my BMW. I was missing the peace of God. *I got tired of being dependent on the world for peace.*

When you're in the world system, you have to do what you don't want to do. You have to say what you don't want to say and go where you don't want to go. You have to act in ways you don't want to act and dress the way you don't want to dress. Your entire happiness is dependent on doing things the way the world's system says they should be done, whether that makes you happy or not. And you find you can't trust people in the world, even when you try to play the political games they think you ought to play.

Unfortunately, an unsaved person is capable of any evil. It doesn't matter how nice they seem to be, if they are unsaved, they are susceptible to being used by the devil. A heart which has not been born again is a heart which is still susceptible to wickedness. And I finally got tired of living with people like that. I got tired of "world" peace. I wanted the real peace which comes only from the Word.

Word peace is not based on anything in the world or on any world system. *Word peace is based on God and on what He said.* Jesus said:

> **...My peace I give unto you: not as the world giveth, give I unto you. Let not your heart be troubled, neither let it be afraid.**

> **JOHN 14:27**

Again, why did Jesus give us peace? So our hearts won't be troubled. The force of peace is what I use to keep my heart from being troubled. The security in the midst of the storm is what I use to **let not my heart be troubled.** And besides that, I use peace to not be afraid. "Word" peace will produce two benefits I can never get from "world" peace: a trouble-free heart and freedom from fear.

How Do I Get Peace?

If "Word" peace can produce for us hearts that are not troubled and hearts that aren't filled with fear, we certainly need to know how to get this kind of peace. I know this peace has been made available to me because Jesus said He gave it to me. But how do I take hold of it? Isaiah 26:3 gives us a clue:

> **Thou wilt keep him in perfect peace, whose mind is stayed on thee: because he trusteth in thee.**

The key word here is *stay*. The one who is kept in peace is not one whose mind just visits once in a while, but one whose mind *stays*. Stays on what? On the Word of God. God and His Word are the same (John 1:1), so if I am going to be stayed on God, I must be stayed on His Word. You cannot separate God from His Word. So my mind has to be stayed, or fixed, on God's Word.

That sounds like meditation on God's Word, doesn't it? It sounds like a lifestyle of paying attention to God's Word. Do you see what your responsibility is in the process of acquiring peace? Peace comes from God's Word. Therefore, in order to get peace, you have to get God's Word. No Word, no peace. No Word of God, no peace of God.

In order to get Word peace, you must get the Word. He'll keep you in perfect peace when your mind is stayed on the Word. Why? **...Because he trusteth in thee.**

I told you in the last chapter that if you're having trouble trusting God, the solution to your problem is to get established in His Word. When you get your mind stayed on the Word, you get your mind in a position where the Word of God is giving you peace and security. And when you have peace and security, you are in a position to overcome trouble.

Don't Let the Devil Steal Your Peace

Now the devil will do his best to steal your peace. "Well, Brother Dollar," you might say, "why would the devil want to steal my peace? It doesn't look like my peace is hurting him." On the contrary, child of God, your peace is big trouble to the devil because Romans 8:6 says:

> **For to be carnally minded is death: but to be spiritually minded is life and peace.**

What is carnal-mindedness? The word *carnal*[1] means "fleshly"; therefore, to be carnally minded means to be fleshly minded, to be world system minded, to be void-of-the-Word minded. And the Bible says to be carnally minded is death. Death is separation from God. So Paul is saying here that to have a mind void of God's Word is to be separated from God. To have a mind of flesh is to be separated from God.

You have no communion with God when you have a mind of the flesh. Carnality, the Bible says, is **enmity against God** (Romans 8:7). You are dead and separated from the things of God when you are carnally minded. **...But to be spiritually minded...**is what? Word-minded. Jesus said:

> **The words that I speak unto you, they are spirit, and they are life.**

> **JOHN 6:63**

So to be spiritually minded is to be Word-minded. And to be spiritually minded *is life and peace.* A mind that is not affected by the Word is a mind that does not have peace.

"Okay," you say, "but what do I do when I don't have peace?" Do what the Bible says to do — **seek peace and pursue it** (Psalm 34:14), that is, pursue the Word. Whenever you lack peace, *stop what you're doing right then and get in the Word.* Don't pace around the room wringing your hands and moaning, "Oh, Jesus, give me peace," because all He can say is, "I've already given it to you." No, no. **Seek, inquire for, and crave peace and pursue (go after) it** (Psalm 34:14, AMP) in the Word. Open your Bible, read it, meditate on it, focus in on it. *Peace is in the Word of God.* If you're looking for peace anywhere except in the Word, you're looking for it in all the wrong places.

So why is the devil after your peace? The Bible says Satan comes immediately to take away the Word that has been sown in your heart (Mark 4:15). But Jesus keeps telling us to let not our hearts be troubled, to hold on to our peace.

Now let me show you why peace is trouble to the devil. *Peace is my security guard. The devil wants to take the Word out of me, but he cannot take the Word from me as long as I refuse to let go of my peace and refuse to let myself be troubled by his trouble.*

Hold On to Your Peace

As long as I have peace, Satan cannot take the Word from me. My peace *holds on to the Word.* My peace says, "I don't care what trouble I'm facing, I will not let go of my peace. It's all I've got. Satan, I'm not going to let you have my peace. You've taken my car. You've taken my house. But I'm not going to let you have my peace, hallelujah! If I can keep my peace, I'll get another car. If I can keep my peace, I'll get another house. If I can keep my peace, I'm coming out of this trouble. I've got to hold on to my peace. It's all I've got left. I've got to know that I know that God is able to do what He said. And I will let that anchor my mind. I'll let peace anchor my soul. I don't care how hard it gets; I don't care how hot it gets; I don't care what the trouble is, I'm not going to let go of my peace. As long as I don't let go of my peace, Satan can't steal the Word out of my heart."

Let me tell you a personal experience which shows how keeping yourself in peace overcomes any kind of trouble the devil throws at you.

One day two pastor friends of mine and I went shopping at a mall close to my home. When we got ready to leave, my car would not start. Immediately, one of my friends began praying and binding devils and rebuking demons, but I said, "Brother, my car doesn't have any demons on it. It just won't crank." So he said, "Well, praise the Lord, let's go get some hamburgers and let the Lord take care of this situation." So we went back into the mall and ate lunch and just refused to let this situation with the car that wouldn't start steal our peace.

After all, this was no big deal. We had security in the midst of this trouble. We had three other cars available in the city. All we had to do was call somebody to come pick up us and have my car taken to a garage to be fixed.

We just ate our lunch while we waited for the people I called to come get us — and through it all we absolutely refused to let the devil steal our peace. Oh, he tried, but we knew we were walking in the peace of God because we had His Word that said He would take care of our every need even in the midst of trouble. And by the time we finished eating, there was another car right outside the door waiting for us.

We changed cars, my car was taken to be repaired, and later that same day, when my friends and I got back to my church, my car was sitting there not only fixed, but washed and vacuumed out.

It's the peace of God that will keep the devil from stealing your peace. He may throw terrible trouble at you, but he can't hurt you if you refuse to let go of the peace which comes from God's Word. In the midst of the worst trouble you can imagine, you can have victory if you refuse to let go of your peace.

Just say, "No, in the name of Jesus, I'm not going to let go of my peace. I'm not going to let go of my Bible. I won't let go because my God is greater than this situation. If I can just hold on to my peace, God will settle this thing. If I can just hold on to my peace, God *has* to bring me out of this trouble. *He has to do it because He swore by Himself.* I have security in the midst of this turmoil. I have a guarantee.

My Jesus said He has given me **power to tread on serpents and scorpions, and over all the power of the enemy: and nothing shall by any means hurt** [me] (Luke 10:19). I won't let go of my peace. It's all I've got. By keeping my peace, I keep my Word. And by keeping my Word, I keep my victory. And my victory brings me out of trouble, glory to God!"

Don't Panic

Many people lose their peace because they panic. They get upset over what hasn't even happened yet. They walk the floor and worry.

"Oh, Lord, what if my boy's at a party doing drugs?" But the boy is home in bed asleep.

"What if they have a wreck in my car?" Your car is parked in the driveway.

"Oh, God, what if I get laid off?" The company you work for has just announced a major expansion in your plant, and they're hiring hundreds of new workers.

Child of God, shut your fearful mouth! You see, sometimes we make things happen by talking negatively. So hold on to the Word of God and hold on to your peace. Don't get upset and make yourself miserable. When you're upset, you play right into the devil's hands. He loves to see you miserable.

But it troubles the devil when you refuse to get upset. When he has thrown some big temptation in your way, and you keep your mind fixed on the Word, he is troubled. You troubled him when he sent a truck load of women by, but you stayed home with your wife. You troubled him when you refused to do drugs at the party. You troubled him when your boss wanted you to do something unethical or illegal at work, and you wouldn't do it.

It troubles every demon in hell when, in spite of everything they throw against you, instead of speaking doubt and unbelief, you say, "It's going to be all right."

When you say that, the devil knows he has a problem. He says, "Oh, oh, I'm in trouble. I threw everything I had against those people, but they're saying 'It's going to be all right.'" That's your peace. That's the spiritual force you're releasing which will make things come out all right. And, you know, most of the time, if you just don't panic and lose your peace, that situation will get resolved, and things really do turn out all right.

Using Your Weapons

The peace which comes from the Word of God is such a powerful force for troubling your trouble and overcoming every trial and temptation Satan puts in your way, you should begin right now using it daily. Confess the following every day:

> In the name of Jesus, I am troubling my trouble. I declare right now that I will see that I be not troubled. I will let not my heart be troubled. I will use the force of peace. I will have security in the midst of turmoil. I will pursue peace. I will live in peace. And the peace of God which

passes all my understanding will sustain me. The Promoter and the Author of peace will be with me.

I thank You, Lord, that because I have my mind stayed on the Word of God, I have the peace of God. In Jesus' name, I am going to hold on to that Word. And by holding on to the Word of God, I will hold on to the peace of God.

No matter what trouble comes, peace will remain because my God has given me a covenant of peace. He has sworn by Himself. His Word is my security, and in His Word I have peace. In Jesus' name. Amen.

[1] James Strong, "Greek Dictionary of the New Testament," *Strong's Exhaustive Concordance of the Bible,* (Nashville: Abingdon, 1890), p. 64, #4561.

4

TROUBLING YOUR TROUBLE
WITH THE FORCE OF PEACE

Part 2: Functions of Peace

━━━━━━━━━━━━━━

We saw in the last chapter that in John 16:33, Jesus placed before us two systems of living. When He said, **These things I have spoken unto you, that in me ye might have peace. In the world ye shall have tribulation: but be of good cheer; I have overcome the world,** He made a contrast between the system of the Word, in which we will have peace, and the system of the world, in which, Jesus says, we will have trouble or tribulation.

I want us to look at this contrast in systems in a little more depth. Knowing which system you are operating in has an important bearing on how well you will be able to maintain your peace in time of trouble.

It's Your Choice

━━━━━━━━━━━━━━

We now have before us, in John 16:33, two contrasting systems of values for operating in life: the system of the Word, and the system of the world. In the Word system we find security and guarantees. In the Word system, we find promises of security in the midst of trouble. In the world system, Jesus promises us, we will find tribulation. He promises us we will find trials. He promises us that we will find trouble.

Now you have to make a choice. You have to choose either the world system or the Word system. But you can't mingle these two systems. You can't try to operate in the Word system one day and in the world system the next and still expect to receive what the Word promises you. So you have to make a decision that you will operate in the Word system, or in the world system. But you cannot operate in both systems, because if you do, I submit to you that you are operating in the system of hypocrites. You're a hypocrite if you don't make a decision to operate in one system or the other.

The World's Head Start

So you're faced with a choice of systems, and like two rival political parties, both the world system and the Word system want you to choose it instead of the other. Both the world and the Word promise you benefits if you choose to live by its system, but unfortunately, in this campaign for your life, the world has a head start.

The world has a head start because your natural birth into the physical world preceded your spiritual rebirth into the kingdom of God. And from the day you were born in the natural world, you have been in preparation to operate in the world's system. You have been educated to operate in the world's system. You have achieved higher learning in operating in the world's system. Depending on how old you are, how much experience you've had with the world, and how well you've learned the lessons life in the world has taught you since you were born, you've become pretty skilled in working the world system.

The amount of success you've had in life is in proportion to how well you've learned to operate in the world system. Maybe your degree, your job, your money and material possessions haven't brought you happiness and peace. But at least you know how to get the things the world values by operating the world system.

But then one day, you find out that you're going to live forever either in heaven or hell. Of course, you want to go to heaven, but you find out the world system in which you've been so well trained won't get you there. So you decide to find out what system to use to get to heaven. You get born again, and start reading the Bible and listening to preaching and teaching on the Word. And you discover the Bible says in four different places, "The just shall live by faith" (Habakkuk 2:4; Romans 1:17; Galatians 3:11; Hebrews 10:38). When you ask what that means, you're told it means that the people who have been born again and translated out of the kingdom of darkness into the kingdom of light, are supposed to live a lifestyle of faith.

A Whole New System

So now the Bible says you've got to learn a whole new system. You have to get educated all over again. You have to "renew your mind" as the Bible calls it. Because what God promises will not work if you do not make a commitment to live by the system. You've spent all your life educating yourself to operate in the world system. But now you have to start over and begin educating yourself in the Word system. Because if you don't *know* about the Word system, then how can you receive from the Word system? If you don't *know* how the Word system works, how can you operate in the Word system?

What does it mean to operate by the Word system? *To operate in the Word system means I conduct my life by God's Word.* I handle my finances by God's Word. I educate myself on what the Word of God says concerning a believer's finances. And I manage my finances according to the Bible's system instead of continuing to operate my finances by the world's system.

When I live under the Word system, I operate my finances by the Word, I raise my children by the Word, I treat my wife or husband by the Word. I speak by the Word. I believe by the Word. My attitude is adjusted by the Word.

Since I now call myself a Christian, I operate according to the system laid out for me in God's Word. I no longer operate in the world system, because the Bible says I can't continue to operate in the world's system and yet expect to receive the results of the Word of God.

One of the Results

As we've already said, one of the results we can expect to receive from living according to the system of God's Word is *peace*. We are Word people who have made a decision to live in the system of the Word and therefore, we have security in the midst of any storm, trouble or turmoil. Trouble does not trouble us — we trouble trouble! Because we have chosen the Word system, we can trouble our trouble with the spiritual force of peace.

But before we can become skillful in using peace as a weapon to overcome trouble, we have to know more about peace and what its functions are. When we find out more about the peace of God, we have a better idea of how to respond to trouble when it comes.

Untroubled Hearts

The first function of peace is to prevent the hearts of God's people from being troubled. In Matthew 24:6, Jesus commanded His disciples, **See that ye be not troubled.** And in Philippians 4:6, Paul exhorts us not to allow anything to cause us to be full of care or worry.

> **Be careful for nothing....**
>
> **And the peace of God, which passeth all understanding, shall keep your hearts and minds through Christ Jesus.**
>
> PHILIPPIANS 4:6,7

The word translated *keep*[1] is a military term in the original Greek. It means to *keep with a military guard.* And the word *Christ* in Greek means *anointed.*[2] Therefore, since we know from John 1:1 that Jesus and the Word are the same, we could paraphrase that verse this way: "The peace of God which passes all understanding shall keep as a military guard your hearts and minds through the anointed Word of God." Seeing it that way makes it easier to apply to our own situations.

I can now use the anointed Word of God as a military guard to keep or guard my mind. As a military guard, it keeps my heart. It may be difficult for me to keep my peace in times of trouble and tribulation, but the anointed Word acts like a military guard to keep my mind stayed on the Word and on the peace of God when trouble comes.

Care Brings Trouble

There's a good reason the Bible warns us not to be full of care, because care [or worry] brings on trouble. However, the Word of God brings peace. We can see how this works in the story of Mary and Martha in Luke 10:38-42.

> **Now it came to pass, as they went, that he entered into a certain village: and a certain woman named Martha received him**

into her house. And she had a sister called Mary, which also sat at Jesus' feet, and heard his word. But Martha was cumbered about much serving, and came to him, and said, Lord, dost thou not care that my sister hath left me to serve alone? bid her therefore that she help me. And Jesus answered and said unto her, Martha, Martha, thou are careful and troubled about many things: But one thing is needful: and Mary hath chosen that good part, which shall not be taken away from her.

LUKE 10:38-42

Why did Jesus chide Martha for being **careful and troubled about many things?** Well, what did we just read about care? The Bible said in Philippians 4:6, **Be careful for *nothing,*** didn't it? But here Martha is full of care, anxiety and trouble. So obviously when you're full of care, you're going to be troubled. You can't be full of care and be free of trouble. What is it that chokes the Word of God? *CARE!* The cares of this world entering in choke the Word of God. And it produces no fruit.

Jesus said, "Martha, you are *care-full* and troubled about many things." So now she's not troubling her trouble, she is filled with care and troubled by those things she's full of care about. But look what Jesus says next.

But one thing is needful: and Mary hath chosen that good part, which shall not be taken away from her.

LUKE 10:42

Spiritual Priorities

Now listen to me, child of God. The first thing that happens to believers when they lack peace and their hearts are troubled is they begin to neglect the most needful part of their lives. Whenever your life is filled with care and trouble, you can be sure you have been neglecting the most needful part of your life.

And the most needful part is not the serving part — the most needful part is the Word part. Mary sat at the feet of Jesus to hear and receive the Word of God. Remember what we said about staying in the Word and developing roots? The Bible says man shall not live by bread alone. It says you need something more than bread to exist. What more do you need? — **every word of God** (Luke 4:4). That's the needful part. We must understand spiritual priorities.

As a pastor, I often see Christians who have gotten in the Word of God and because of the Word, they're propelled into wanting to serve God. They've spent time in the Word of God, and the Word has created in them a desire to serve in some area of ministry.

But all too often, after they've been in some area of service — choir or ushering or teaching a Bible class or some other ministry in their church — for a while, their service for God becomes more important to them than their time spent in God's Word. And then typically, when they stop sitting at the feet of Jesus and eating the Word of God, their service becomes filled with murmuring, with complaining. Their servanthood is not as graced, not as anointed, not as cheerful, as it was when they were spending more time in the Word. Their ministry becomes a burden, and they do things at the church out of obligation and without a revelation.

Because they haven't been sitting at the feet of Jesus and developing deep roots in His Word, their servanthood is filled with care and trouble, and they no longer have peace about serving. Now they're upset about how things are done in the ministry of the church, and before you know it, the devil can run them clear away from the fellowship, because they got angry at someone else in the church who wouldn't help them serve.

But when you're spending time in God's Word, and time comes to do something at the church, you're not going to complain about it even if you're the only person who shows up. You won't complain, because you have been doing the most needful part — sitting at the feet of Jesus and hearing His Word. You count it a double pleasure to be there by yourself to perform your service for the Lord, because you got your spiritual priorities right by putting the Word before your service.

The Perfect Solution

It is not only in service that people become full of care and troubled if they're not spending enough time in the Word. I've learned when people come in for counseling, they're ready to talk about their problems. "Oh, may I help you today?" "Oh, yes, Pastor, let me see, let me start at the beginning." "No, you let me start. Let me ask you a question. How's your Word time?" "Ah, well, ah, you know, okay, it could be better." "Hmmm. How's your prayer time?" "Ahhh, you know, it could be better."

Aha! We've already found the answer to your problem! We don't need to talk about your problem specifically. We've already gotten the root. You're not praying and getting in the Word. Now why should you waste my time and your time coming in to ask me to help you solve your problem, when you're not doing the needful part? If you're not spending time in the Word and praying, you're not operating in the Word system. You want to bring the pastor a worldly problem, one that was gained by operating in the world system, and you want him to give you some godly counsel about how to handle your operation in the world system. No, no, no. Let's clear the problem up at the very beginning.

Do something about your Word time, do something about your prayer time, and then if you *still* need to see the pastor, come back. Don't expect the pastor or the counselor to solve your problem for you when you're not doing what you're supposed to do. Because you're neglecting the most needful part — sitting at the feet of Jesus and hearing His Word — you're careful and troubled about many things. But, child of God, if you continue to neglect God's Word, if you continue to neglect prayer, I can give you all the right answers to your problem, but none of them will work for you until you make a decision to live in God's Word.

Until you get your spiritual priorities straight and make an irreversible decision to operate in the Word system and not in the world system, you'll continue to be defeated by trouble. You'll be stuck in a vicious circle — the more care and trouble you let into your life, the more the Word will be choked out of it, and the more you neglect the Word, the more careful and troubled you'll be. Remember, the Word of God and the peace which comes from it are there to guard and keep your mind and heart like a military guard. If you will concentrate on the needful part of sitting at the feet of Jesus and hearing His Word, if you'll get your priorities right and put the Word before your service, the peace of God which passes understanding will guard your heart and mind through the anointed Word.

The Built-In Compass

The second function of peace is *to determine direction in the life of the earnest believer*. To determine direction. How many times have you gone to the Lord and said, "Lord, do You really want me to do this? Or do You really want me to go this way?" Or, "Lord, what is it that You want me to do?" Or, "Lord, are You saying this?" Or, "Lord, are You saying that?" Or, "Lord, should I give this?" Or, "Lord, should I hold this?" Or, "Lord, should I say this?" How many times have you had to face that dilemma? We get into that dilemma because we have not recognized that God has built into the spirit of every born-again Christian, a direction compass device called *peace.*

God uses the fruit of peace to guide the steps of His children so that their lives will be in keeping with His perfect plan and purpose. That's one of the ways He uses His peace. I want you to pay close attention to what I'm saying here, because this could change your life. If you're having problems hearing from God, you can learn how to depend on this built-in security system that God has put on the inside of every born-again believer. Every born-again believer has a built-in security system, a built-in direction finder. And that security system and direction finder is called *peace.*

This function of peace is explained in Colossians 3:15:

> **And let the peace of God rule in your hearts, to the which also you are called in one body; and be ye thankful.**

Now notice the word *let.* That means it is my responsibility to let peace rule. In order to benefit from this security system which is built into me, I have to *let* it work. **And let the peace of God *rule....*** The word *rule* in the Greek means *to act as an umpire or to arbitrate or to decide.* When there is a question of direction, the peace of God is to be the deciding factor in a believer's heart.

The Amplified Bible makes this function of the peace of God even clearer:

> **And let the peace (soul harmony which comes) from Christ rule (act as an umpire continually) in your hearts [deciding and settling with finality all questions that arise in your minds, in that peaceful state] to which as [members of**

Christ's] one body you were also called [to live]. And be thankful (appreciative), [giving praise to God always].

COLOSSIANS 3:16, AMP

I want you to pay particular attention to the phrase, **deciding and settling with finality all questions that arise in your minds.** When you are in doubt and have questions in your mind about which way to go on an issue, the peace of God will decide the matter for you if you know how to let it work. Sometimes it's the *lack of peace in your heart* that will give you the clue that you're going in the wrong direction. Let me give some examples to illustrate this principle.

Don't Overrule the Umpire!

Have you ever been in a business meeting or listening to a presentation, and even though everything about the proposed course of action seems just right on the surface, even though the words are right and the numbers are right, questions arise in your mind? You can't put your finger on what's wrong with the situation, but you just don't "feel right" about it. Even though everyone else in the meeting is all for doing whatever it is, inside you're uneasy about it for no visible reason.

Child of God, when that happens, when you get that uneasy feeling inside that says you don't have peace about what's going on, you need to run to the nearest exit! Because that is the peace of God inside you acting as an umpire to tell you, "Something's wrong. There's deception here. There's danger here. Whoa. Watch out. Better get out of here." And if you don't listen to that inner umpire, if you overrule its decisions, you'll wind up in trouble.

Later, you'll be shaking your head and saying, "Something told me not to do that."

Learning to operate in this function of peace would save many good Christian people from making mistakes about marriage partners. Sometimes a man looks at a woman or a woman looks at a man, and everything about that potential mate just seems to *look* perfect. The woman checks out the man and finds out he's got a good job, he's got a nice car, he treats her nicely when they go out, takes her to nice places, acts like the perfect gentleman, answers all her questions just like she dreamed he would — everything seems to be so right. And yet, for no reason she can determine except she doesn't "feel right" about it, she doesn't want to marry him. She even loves him, but "something" on the inside of her is telling her to leave him alone.

If she's been taught to operate in the peace of God, she'll listen to that inner umpire and wait until a more suitable mate comes along. She'll wait until she finds the man God intends for her to marry, and she'll know who he is immediately because inside she'll be all calm and peaceful — she'll know this man is the right one because the peace of God is all over the relationship.

The Price of Not Letting Peace Rule

But if she chooses to go contrary to the direction of the inner umpire, she may wind up in a bad marriage. Oh, things may go all right at first. They get married, have a fancy wedding, have a romantic honeymoon in the Bahamas — everything seems to be so right. And she begins to wonder if she just imagined being uneasy about marrying him. But now she's operating in the peace we often make up in our own minds. Instead of being God's peace, it's a peace that says everything's all right just because we want it to be. And soon after they get home from the honeymoon, her husband comes in one day acting crazy, and she finds out he's quit his job, wrecked the car, and now all he wants to do is just lie around on the couch all day and watch wrestling on television. Now the marriage is in trouble; they're both miserable, and it's all because they didn't know how to let the peace of God rule in their hearts before they got married.

The peace of God, the built-in security system that is inside every born-again believer, will always work if you let it. It will get your attention every time, but if you don't know what it is, if you don't identify it as God's guidance system, you may ignore it. And if you ignore the warnings of the inner umpire, you will end up going contrary to what you know in your heart is right. Peace is designed to lead you in the right direction. But God never forces you to go His way. His peace will lead you, but you have to *let* it rule in your heart.

It's Our Responsibility

The force of peace is a powerful weapon God has given us to trouble our trouble, and to guide us in making the right decisions in our lives. But having peace already given us by God won't benefit us if we don't do our part by *learning how* to operate in the system of God's Word, and then *making a decision* to operate that way in every area of our lives. A weapon will only benefit you if you use it.

Jesus has given us everything we need to overcome trouble, but it's our responsibility to claim these things by faith and use them in our lives. Peace is available to give us security in the midst of every storm. However, the storm won't cease if we just stand around like the apostles in Mark 4:38, wringing our hands and saying, "Oh, Lord Jesus, don't You care that we're about to sink?" The Prince of Peace was right there in the boat, but the storm didn't cease until He got up and *said,* **Peace, be still** (Mark 4:39). Then He asked the disciples:

Why are ye so fearful? how is it that ye have no faith?

Mark 4:40

In other words, why didn't *you* use your peace? Why didn't *you* speak to the storm and tell it to be still? Why did you let your hearts be troubled? Why didn't you trouble your trouble with the force of peace?

Of course, Jesus knew it would not be easy to stand still on the Word when everything is going to pieces around you. When you're going through your hardest time in life, when trouble is all around you, in your finances, in your marriage, in your family — sometimes your peace wants to do a "moon walk" and leave you. Remember, the devil is trying to steal your peace so he can steal the Word out of your heart.

But it's in those times when the hurricane of trouble is roaring around you that you have to be sure to do the needful part. It's then that you have to grab your Bible, open it up to the Scriptures that speak to your particular storm, and say, "Word of God that I stand on, be still. Word of God, I'm not letting you get away from me. I won't let this storm drive the Word out of me. I will hold onto this Word. I will keep my mind stayed and fixed on this Word. I will stand still on this Word. And as long as the Word is still in me, all the trouble around me will have to settle down. It will have to stop. It will have to go into a calm. Trouble, I speak to you in the name of Jesus and say, Peace, be still."

Child of God, when you feel like you're in a hurricane, get your Bible and look at what Jesus said.

Peace, be still. And the wind ceased, and there was a great calm.

MARK 4:39

Even in the natural, in every hurricane there is an *eye of the storm*. In the center of every storm there is a place of calm where you can be still. The storm can be going on around you, but in that place of calm, it can't touch you. That center of calm is the Word of God. It's the place of security in the midst of trouble that comes from holding on to the words Jesus has spoken.

Not Just Any Words

I know it's difficult sometimes to believe that all this power can be in words. But remember, these are not just any old words. The Bible is the anointed, faith-filled Word of God that has been tried and proved. It's been tried and tested and has proven to work every time in every situation. It is absolute security because God swore it to be true, and God can't lie. It's an unbreakable covenant. So any time you are going through trouble, and you can find out what God has to say about that particular type of trouble, you have security in the midst of that trouble.

That's why you can't afford to be without the Word when the doctors are telling you you're going to die next week. When they give you that bad report, go get the Word of God. It's your security that healing is available to you as an heir of salvation. You can't afford to be without the Word when your marriage is on the rocks. That's when you need to get on *the Rock* and stand on Jesus and

His Word. Because when you find security in God's Word, you've found the guarantee that what God said will come to pass and what the world said won't.

The Faith of Abraham

That's what Abraham did. God told him he was going to have a baby, even though he was nearly 100 years old and his wife had been barren all her life. The world said, "You can't." But Abraham said, "God said I can, and I'm going to hold onto what God said. I'm going to be still right here, standing on God's Word until the answer comes." The world scoffed at Abraham and Sarah for years, but finally Isaac was born. In the face of all that the world had predicted, only what God said would come to pass actually came to pass. Abraham overcame trouble because he made a decision to operate in the Word of God system, and to trouble his trouble with the force of peace.

As the seed of Abraham and joint heirs with Jesus Christ, we have everything we need to let not our hearts be troubled, and to let the peace of God rule in our hearts. Confessing God's Word out loud will help you keep your mind stayed on the source of peace.

In the name of Jesus, I make a decision now to use the force of peace. My heart will not be troubled. It is my responsibility to see that I be not troubled and to hold on to the Word of God. And by holding on to the Word of God, I hold on to the peace of God. I guard my mind and my heart with the peace of God, and I declare now that I will no longer ignore the built-in security system called peace. Peace is my umpire. Peace is my friend, and peace will direct me into the place of calm with God.

I declare right now in the midst of trouble, "Peace, be still." In my finances, "Peace, be still." In my marriage, "Peace, be still." In every area of my life, "Peace, be still." A great calm comes over my life. In Jesus' name. Amen.

[1] James Strong, "Greek Dictionary of the New Testament," *Strong's Exhaustive Concordance of the Bible,* (Nashville: Abingdon, 1890), p. 76, #5432.

[2] Ibid., p. 78, #5547.

5

How to Trouble Your Trouble
With the Force of Joy

Throughout this book we've been emphasizing that being a born-again Christian does not mean you will be free of trouble. Walking by faith does not mean you will be free of trouble. Jesus told us in John 16:33 that trouble, that trials and tribulation, will come. As long as we are physically in the world, surrounded by the world system, we can expect to be subjected to trouble.

But Jesus also said that although trouble will come, it does not have to overcome. He said:

> **In the world ye shall have tribulation:** *but be of good cheer;* **I have overcome the world.**

> **JOHN 16:33**

We've already learned that as joint heirs with Christ, we can overcome trouble because Jesus has overcome it. In the previous two chapters we've learned how to use the fruit of the spirit of peace to trouble our trouble. But peace is not the only spiritual force Jesus has given us to use against trouble. He tells us what other spiritual force is in His command: **But be of good cheer.** Another word for *cheer* is *joy*.

The Source of Joy

Now we need to pay particular attention to the context of what Jesus said here. He said, **In the *world* you shall have tribulation**

but.... Notice the word *but*. That word introduces a contrast. "In the world," Jesus said, "you will be subjected to trouble, *but* be of good cheer...." Even in the world where we are going through trouble and tribulation, we are to be of good cheer. In spite of all the trouble we're in, we are to have joy.

If Jesus is saying, "Be of good cheer in the midst of trouble," then that must mean there are benefits to being of good cheer. That must mean I will benefit in some way when I am of good cheer even when I'm in trouble. That must mean I can use good cheer or joy in some way to affect my trouble. That must mean I can trouble my trouble with the force of joy.

"But, Brother Dollar," you may say, "when I'm in trouble, I sure don't feel very joyful. Where is this joy going to come from?" Jesus tells us in John 15:

> **If you keep my commandments, ye shall abide in my love; even as I have kept my Father's commandments, and abide in his love.**

> **JOHN 15:10**

Overcoming Emotions

Now let me say something about this verse which illustrates an important point. *It is vitally important that we read God's Word to get what God has to say on every subject.* For example, without the Word of God, I would never really know what love is. Without understanding what God's Word says about love, I would think as most people do that love is an emotion. But if love were an emotion, when my emotions change — and they change minute by minute — then my love will change too.

But in John 15:10, the Bible says love comes when you keep God's commandments, when you abide in His commandments. *Abide*[1] means "to set up residence" there; it means to live there. *To abide* does not mean to go in and out at your convenience. It means to live there.

Jesus says, "When you keep my commandments, you love me." *Therefore, love is based on obedience, not on emotion.* "Do what I tell you to do," He said, "and you demonstrate My love."

Now when I get that Word and deposit it in my heart, especially in my marriage, then I know how to overcome my emotions. So when I don't *feel* like I love any more, I simply obey God where the Word tells me to be the type of husband I need to be. I simply obey God, and my wife simply obeys God, and whatever love we *thought* we lost will be rekindled as we obey God. That's called submitting yourselves one to another. As we are obeying God and doing what the Word tells us to do, whatever we thought we'd lost, we'll find out we really gained.

But I can never do that if I don't know what the Word says. So knowing what the Word says becomes vital to my marriage. As we've said over and over in this book, I have to *know* what the Word of God says in order to use it to overcome trouble in any area of my life.

Joy From the Spoken Word

Jesus goes on to say:

These things have I spoken unto you, that my joy might remain in you, and that your joy might be full.

JOHN 15:11

Just as He said, **These things I have spoken unto you, that...ye might have peace** (John 16:33), He now says, **These things have I spoken unto you...that your joy might be full.** Therefore, *joy comes from hearing what Jesus said. Joy comes from the spoken Word.*

"I thought peace comes from the Word," you say. Yes, you're exactly right. Peace comes from the spoken Word. Love comes from the spoken Word. Longsuffering comes from the spoken Word. The fruit of the Spirit comes from the spoken Word. No Word, no peace. No Word, no love. No Word, no joy. No Word, no fruit of the Spirit.

Somebody says, "I want to be like Jesus." No Word, no being like Jesus. Because what is Jesus like? The Word. Somebody says, "I'm a born-again Christian." No Word, no born-again Christian. Listen to me, child of God, anybody can say they're a born-again Christian, but they won't bear the fruit of their righteousness if they're not getting in the Word of God.

Known by the Fruit

You can ask a person "Are you a Christian?" They say, "Yes," but then you look at their life, and see they are bearing no fruit. You may say, "What difference does that make?" But it makes all the difference in the world because the Bible says a tree can be identified by the fruit it bears.

Therefore, when you say you are a Christian, I first want to test that assertion by looking at what kind of fruit is coming off your branch. You can claim to be born again. But if you're going around looking like a whipped dog all the time and moaning and groaning about how much trouble you're in, I have reason to wonder whether you're really born again or not.

Jesus said, "I have spoken these things to you that you might have my joy." Remember how He said in John 14:27, **My peace I give unto you....** Now He says He has given us His joy. The words Jesus has spoken have given us Jesus' own joy.

Joy Gives Strength

Now what benefit will having Jesus' joy be to me in troubling my trouble? I know Jesus intended it to benefit me because He said, "I left it for you." He said, "I've spoken these things so that you can have my joy and that your joy might be full." So Jesus must expect us to live with a full tank of joy. But what is the significance of living with joy? The Bible tells us the importance of joy in Nehemiah 8.

> **So they read in the book in the law of God distinctly, and gave the sense, and caused them to understand the reading.**
>
> **And Nehemiah, which is the Tirshatha, and Ezra the priest the scribe, and the Levites that taught the people, said unto all the people, This day is holy unto the Lord your God; mourn not, nor weep. For all the people wept, when they heard the words of the law. Then he said unto them, Go your way, eat the fat, and drink the sweet, and send portions unto them for whom nothing is prepared: for this day is holy unto our Lord: neither be ye sorry; for the joy of the Lord is your strength.**
>
> **NEHEMIAH 8:8-10**

Since Nehemiah says, **The joy of the Lord is your strength** in verse 10, the implication is that there is a correlation between what he says in verse 10 and what happened in verses 8 and 9.

What happened in verses 8 and 9? Ezra and the other priests read the Word of God to the people and explained to them what it meant. Then the people wept for joy because somebody finally made sense of the Word of God.

I Didn't Understand One Word!

I'm sure many of you have read the Bible at some point in your life, just as I have, and did not understand anything it was saying. Of course, it's easier to understand the Word after you're saved. But even saved, I've read certain portions of the Bible over and over at times and still not understood a word of it. And I have gone to a church service where the preacher seemed to be preaching brilliantly, but I still didn't understand anything he was saying. I was as confused when I left as I was when I came in. Nothing really happened to me spiritually from hearing the Word preached because I didn't understand one word of the sermon.

But something happened here when the **book in the law of God** (v. 8) was read aloud to the people. The Bible was read aloud, and somebody explained its meaning. Somebody caused the hearers to understand the reading. And what happened? **All the people wept** (v. 9).

Can you recall the first time you understood something out of the Bible? Can you recall the first time you heard a sermon and understood what the man was talking about? All of a sudden, something began to happen on the inside of you because you understood. Suddenly you understood what it meant to pray in the name of Jesus rather than to pray "for Christ's sake". You understood what it means to walk in authority over demons and devils.

You understood what it was like to be the head and not the tail, above and never again beneath.

You understood how to be the man of your house instead of the wimp of your house.

You understood how to be a submissive wife instead of a Jezebel wife.

You understood. And the Bible says **for all the people wept, when they heard the words of the law.**

I Wept

I'll never forget the first time I heard a sermon I thought God had arranged to have preached specifically for me. I was getting ready to go to a ministers' conference, but before I left I was trying to decide how to handle a very odd and troubling situation in my church. I went to the Lord about what I should do to solve this problem, but He told me not to do anything until after the conference. And when I got there, I realized why.

At the conference, what a friend of mine, Mac Hammond, was preaching from the Word was exactly what my wife and I needed to hear to handle the problem we had at our church. As I sat there listening to the preaching of the Word, tears started coming out of my eyes...because I understood. I thought, *It makes sense now. Now, I understand it, Lord.*

And I realized God loves me. God is concerned about me. God loves me so much that He would get somebody to make sense of something that didn't make any sense to me before. I wept with joy, because I finally understood how God's Word applied to me personally.

So I now understand this Scripture. I understand why the people of God wept when they first heard the Word and understood it.

Joy Equals Strength

However, Nehemiah told the people not to mourn. He told them to celebrate because **the joy of the Lord is your strength** (v. 10). Now if I remove the phrase **of the Lord,** the statement would read "joy is your strength." Joy equals your strength. What joy? Jesus' joy equals your strength.

Where did the joy come from in this Scripture? From hearing the Word of God. When you get the Word, you get joy. It's when you understand the Word of God that the joy of the Lord has been made available to you. And when you get joy, you get strength. And when you're strong, you can win. And when you win, the devil can't win. And when the devil can't win, he can't steal the Word that has been sown in your heart. If he can't steal the Word, he can't steal your peace, because peace comes from the Word. And if he can't steal the Word, he can't steal your joy, because joy also comes from the Word.

Joy in the Midst of Trouble

What is the relationship of joy to trouble? It may seem like the last place you'd expect to be joyful would be in trouble, but the Bible tells us that's exactly where we ought to be joyful. James 1 says:

> **My brethren, count it all joy when you fall into divers temptations;**
>
> **Knowing this....**
>
> **JAMES 1:2,3**

When do I count it all joy? In the middle of trouble! That's right. When I fall into various temptations, tests and trials, when they cut my lights off, when they lay me off my job, when the doctor says I've got only three weeks to live, I do what? Count it all joy.

"But, Brother Dollar," you're probably saying, "I don't see how being joyful is going to overcome trouble. Even supposing I could do it, how is being joyful going to help me defeat the devil?"

Well, what does the devil expect you to do in the midst of trouble? When you lose your job, he doesn't want you to count it all joy. He wants you to step back and say, "Where was God when all this happened? I mean, God, if you loved me, how come You let me lose my job?" That's what he wants you to do.

But it confuses all of hell when you count it all joy in the middle of trouble.

What do you think you look like to the devil when you're dancing on the side of the road where your car just broke down? People are going by saying, "What's wrong with that idiot? What is he doing?" Now you may look like an idiot in the natural, but in the realm of the Spirit, God's working something out for you.

It's Not Necessary to Be Happy!

Count it all joy when you fall into trouble or into various temptations, tests or trials. "Hmm," you say, "that's not easy to do." You may think it's hard to do because you're not too happy when you're in trouble. Well, the Bible didn't say count it *happiness*. The Bible says count it *joy*. There's a difference between joy and happiness. Happiness is based on your comfort.

For instance, on a day when it's a hundred degrees in the shade, I'm happy when I'm in a swimming pool, sipping on a glass of cold lemonade. I'm happy because I'm comfortable. I have comfort; I feel good; nothing's bothering me, so I'm happy.

But joy is not based on your comfort. Joy is based on what you know. Look what the Bible says here.

> **My brethren, count it all joy when ye fall into divers temptations;**
>
> *Knowing this....*
>
> JAMES 1:2,3

You have to know something in order to have joy. When I *know* that eventually the new parking lot at our church will be finished and paved, I don't mind parking on the dirt in the meantime. I don't mind because I know parking on the dirt won't last always.

> **Weeping may endure for a night, but joy cometh in the morning.**
>
> PSALM 30:5

I can have joy because I know something. I know something when the rent's overdue and they tell me that I'm going be put out of my house. That looks like trouble, but I know I have financial seed in the ground, and I know my God will supply all of my needs according to His riches in glory. I also know God will never allow me to be forsaken. I know God is with me always. When you know that, you have joy.

And when you know that, you have strength. Now you may not be happy, but I tell you what, when you start living in what you know from the Word of God, your joy will make you happy.

Joy comes from what you know when the doctor tells you you're about to die, but you know that by His stripes you are healed (1 Peter 2:24). Joy comes from what you know when the psychiatrist tells you you're psychotic, but you know that God has given you a sound mind (2 Timothy 1:7). If you're rooted and grounded in the Word of God, you can have joy even when you come home from work one day and find someone has broken into your house and stolen everything you own. If you hold onto what you know from the Word, you can have joy even when you have more trouble and affliction now than you ever imagined having back in the old days before you got saved.

When the Light Comes On

You may not believe you can be joyful in the midst of trouble, but the Bible says it's true. The book of Hebrews says you can have the worst possible trouble yet still take everything joyfully.

> **But call to remembrance the former days, in which, after ye were illuminated, ye endured a great fight of afflictions;**
>
> **Partly, whilst ye were made a gazingstock both by reproaches and afflictions; and partly, whilst ye became companions of them that were so used.**
>
> **For ye had compassion of me in my bonds, and took joyfully the spoiling of your goods, knowing in yourselves that ye have in heaven a better and an enduring substance.**
>
> **HEBREWS 10:32-34**

Do you remember what your life was like in the days right after you first started to get a little understanding of the Word, after you started to be illuminated? Illumination is the shedding of light.

When you're illuminated, light comes on or understanding comes. Remember what happened after you were illuminated, after you understood? You **endured a great fight of afflictions.** You had double and triple trouble. If your experience was anything like mine, it seemed like the devil invented some new kinds of trouble just to use on you. Do you remember that?

All of a sudden, you started learning and understanding the Word, and these fights that you hadn't ever had, that you hadn't even imagined, showed up. Before you were born again, you never saw some of the things you see now. You never saw so much jealousy and envy and strife, so many financial problems, so many family problems, so much opposition from friends and co-workers and, sad to say, from other Christians as you see now. And you think, *What's going on here? All I did was start reading the Bible and understanding a little of it. Why did that bring on all these fights and afflictions?*

What Brought That On?

Well, we know why they come, don't we? We know what the fight is trying to do.

What are the fights of afflictions trying to do? Of course — they're trying to steal the Word from you. After you're illuminated, then the fight comes. After you've found out that you don't have to be poor, then the fight comes. After you find out that you don't have to die of sickness and disease, then the fight comes.

After you find out that you don't have to be stuck in addiction, then the fight comes. After you find out you can be delivered from any danger, then the fight comes. Why does the fight come? Because the devil is trying to keep you where you are.

The devil wants to contain you where you are. If he can convince you that what you've heard is not true, he can keep you from going on with the Lord and learning how to use the Word to defeat trouble. The greatest fear that the devil can put on the Body of Christ is the fear that God's Word is not true.

Therefore, when you hear and understand the Word, Satan's job is to contradict what you've heard. If you fall for his lies, you may be persuaded the Word doesn't mean what it says, and you'll give it up. Then he can keep you in addiction, keep you in bondage and keep you in fear. He can get you into a place where he can continue to bring afflictions and trouble into your life. That's what the Bible says happened to the Hebrew Christians. In the early days, they endured great fights of affliction.

A Better Substance

But how did these born-again believers respond to their trouble? The Bible says they took *joyfully* **the spoiling of your** [their] **goods** (v. 34). Now how is that possible? How in the world can anybody take the spoiling of their goods with joy? How is it that I can be joyful when I come home and find out somebody just broke into my house and stole all of my furniture and everything else I own? How can I take that joyfully? How can I take the death of a loved one joyfully? How can I take losing my job or my business joyfully? In short, how can I take any kind of trouble joyfully?

The Word tells me how:

> ...**knowing in yourselves that ye have in heaven a better and an enduring substance.**
>
> **HEBREWS 10:34**

Knowing...there it is! It's what you *know* that determines whether or not you have joy. You see, if I know that the Word says the thief who stole my goods will be made to restore sevenfold what he stole (Proverbs 6:31), then I can take the theft joyfully because I know God will make the devil — who, of course, is the ultimate thief — restore to me seven times what I had before.

If I know that my dead loved one was born again, Holy Ghost-filled, fire-baptized, I can face the temporary loss joyfully. I know that one day the trump of God will sound and the dead in Christ shall rise, and they that are alive and remain shall be changed in a moment, in the twinkling of an eye, and shall be *caught up together with them* to meet the Lord in the air, and so shall they ever be with the Lord (1 Thessalonians 4:16, 17; 1 Corinthians 15:51, 52). That's why Jesus said:

> **Let not your heart be troubled....In my Father's house are many mansions: if it were not so, I would have told you. I go to prepare a place for you. And if I go and prepare a place for you, I will come again, and receive you unto myself; that where I am, there ye may be also.**

> **JOHN 14:1-3**

Don't Let Trouble Get You Down

No, I'm not going to get down and out because I lose a loved one or someone who was born again dies.

Why?

Because I know what the Bible says about the resurrection of the saints. I know I can look forward to meeting my loved one in heaven one of these days. Hallelujah!

So while someone else is weeping and wailing because "Grandma is gone," I'm rejoicing because I know Grandma was born again. I know she's dead in Christ, and she's already in the mansion Jesus prepared for her in heaven. I can rejoice because of what I know.

I suspect that for years many of you could not have joy because you didn't know anything about the Word of God. You let the bill collectors get you down because you didn't know what the Word says about finances. You let the media tell you there's a recession, and you got down because you didn't know that God promised He would supply all your needs in spite of what's going on in the world economy. Because you didn't know what belongs to you as an heir of salvation, you let the bad reports in the news about down-sizing and layoffs put fear in your heart that you were going to lose your job.

But now that you're illuminated and understand what you read in the Word, you don't pay attention to the recession; you don't participate in a recession because you know that your God shall supply all *your* need according to His riches in glory (Philippians 4:19). You can rest in the joy of the Lord because you know you have an unbreakable covenant. You can rejoice because you're a tither and you know God has promised to rebuke the devourer for your sake (Malachi 3:11). You have treasure laid up in heaven where nobody can steal it (Matthew 6:20). And you rejoice even in the midst of the spoiling of your goods because you know you have in heaven **a better and an enduring substance** (Hebrews 10:34).

The joy of the Lord is your strength in time of trouble. And joy comes from what you know of the Word of God.

Come to the Table

Joy is a powerful weapon against trouble. With the joy that comes from knowing your benefits as a born-again believer and a member of Club *Soteria,* you can take back all the territory and all the goods the devil has stolen from you. The only reason most believers don't get back what's been stolen from them is they don't know they can get it back. Child of God, not only can you take back what the devil has stolen, but you can go to where Satan has hidden it and get it.

That's right — you can go into the enemy's camp.

"How can I do that?" you ask.

By knowing what the Bible says. The Bible says God has prepared a table before us *in the presence of our enemies* (Psalm 23:5). Right in the midst of the enemy's camp God has prepared a table on which He has placed everything I need for nourishment.

Right in the midst of sickness and disease, healing has been prepared on the table. Poverty is in the enemy's camp, but prosperity is prepared for me on the table. Bondage and habit and addiction are there, but deliverance has been prepared on the table. Danger is all around, but protection is waiting for you on the table.

You've been putting up with great fights of afflictions because you didn't *know* that you had a right to sit at the table. You've been under the table trying to get the crumbs that fall off. But now that you *know* you are an heir of God and joint heir with Christ Jesus, it's time for you to get off the floor, sit at the table and eat like a king's kid.

The table is prepared. God is waiting for His children to come to the table. Child of God, it's time you quit letting trouble and affliction overcome you. Rise up in the joy of the Lord. Get up off the floor and take your seat at the table. Get in the Word and learn what it promises you now that you're born again. Sure, trouble and great fights of afflictions will continue to come, but **be strong in the Lord, and in the power of his might** (Ephesians 6:10). Remember, **the joy of the Lord is your strength** (Nehemiah 8:10). When trouble comes, rejoice — *knowing this:* Just because trouble comes, it doesn't have to overcome! When trouble shows up, laugh in its face and say:

> In the name of Jesus, I have joy. Weeping may endure for the night, but joy cometh in the morning. I declare right now I live in joy. The joy of the Lord is my strength. The more Word I get, the more joy I'll have. And the joy of the Lord is my strength. I will eat at the table that has been prepared for me in the presence of my enemies. What has been stolen shall be returned. In Jesus' name, the devil will have to give back to me sevenfold of what he stole from me. Now in the name of Jesus let the return begin. From this point on, I will trouble my trouble with joy. In Jesus' name. Amen.

---

[1] James Strong, "Greek Dictionary of the New Testament," *Strong's Exhaustive Concordance of the Bible,* (Nashville: Abingdon, 1890), p. 47, #3306.

6

Troubling Your Trouble
With the Force of Love

Part 1: The Priorities of Love

So far in this book we've been learning to trouble our trouble with the forces of joy and peace. We've said these forces, like all the fruit of the Spirit, come from the Word of God. We've said we can put them to work in our lives as weapons against trouble only when we develop deep roots in the Word. Only as we learn what the Word teaches us about our position as born again children of God will we be able to overcome trouble and tribulation.

But there is another weapon available to us in our fight against trouble that is even more powerful than the weapons of joy and peace. In fact, this fruit of the Spirit is the most powerful force the world has ever known. It's a weapon that the Bible says will never fail to conquer anything the world, the flesh or the devil can bring against us. This most powerful weapon is *the force of love*.

The Proper Order

In the list of the fruit of the Spirit in Galatians 5:22 and 23, Paul puts love first. It is of great significance that love is listed first. Love is the motivating force behind all the other fruit of the Spirit. Love is the force that will keep you out of the works of the flesh enumerated in Galatians 5:19-21. Love will keep you out of such sins as envy, jealousy, strife, hatred, wrath and so forth. And when you stay out of all these manifestations of the flesh and the world system, you won't be troubled by anything the devil can throw at you.

However, love isn't just a force to keep you out of sin. It's a powerful force to enable you to operate in the other fruit of the Spirit. Without love your joy and peace, your longsuffering, gentleness, goodness, your faith, meekness and temperance won't work. In fact, Paul says in 1 Corinthians 13 that without love, **I am nothing** (v. 2).

You see, if a believer doesn't understand the fruit of love and how to operate in it, he may try to have joy, but his joy won't work properly. He may search for peace, but what he finds won't be true peace. And he won't be able to use peace properly. The same is true of the other fruit of the Spirit. That's why so few Christians are having the kind of success they should have in walking in the Spirit. They don't understand how to operate in the fruit of love. And the major reason they don't know how to operate in love is that they have a misconception about the order of priorities in the love walk. They have a misunderstanding of what the Bible says is the right order of our love relationships. They've mixed up the proper order of priorities in their love life.

The Great Commandment

The trouble is, when most believers think of the fruit of love, they think of cultivating and developing love relationships towards their brothers and sisters in Christ. They think what Jesus called the "great commandment" is His command in John 15:17 **that ye love one another.** But, in fact, the great commandment *is not* **love one another.** The great commandment is not in John 15 but in the book of Matthew. When a lawyer asked Him which was the great commandment in the law, Jesus answered:

Thou shalt love the Lord thy God with all thy heart, and with all thy soul, and with all thy mind. This is the first and great commandment. And the second is like unto it, Thou shalt love thy neighbour as thyself.

MATTHEW 22:37-39

So, according to Jesus, what is the great commandment? *That you love the Lord your God with all your heart and your soul and your mind.* The great commandment is about loving God, not about loving others. The great commandment is not to love one another — it's to love God. It's the *second* commandment that deals with loving others. **Thou shalt love thy neighbor as thyself** (Matthew 22:39). Now you may be surprised, but these two Scriptures put the love life in proper priority.

The Number One Priority

First of all, I must learn to love God with everything that's in me. Secondly, I must learn how to love myself. If I don't know how to love God, I will never know how to love myself. And if I don't get to the point of loving myself, I'll never know how to love another. I cannot love my neighbor as myself until I learn how to love myself. A lot of people are trying to find out what love is all about, but you'll never really find out what love is all about until you get your love life in the right order. And the right order, the right priority, for love life — for any life of love — must begin with God.

So we're talking about loving the Lord as the number one priority. We're talking about cultivating and developing an individual, personal love relationship with your heavenly Father. When you learn to love your heavenly Father, you can learn how to love yourself. And when you learn to love God and yourself, *then* you'll know how to develop love and proper loving relationships with one another.

For instance, what the man who's thinking of committing suicide because he does not love himself must do in order to straighten that situation out, is to develop and cultivate a love relationship with the Almighty God. When he does that, God, through that relationship, can teach him how to love himself. Do you see that?

No Love Life Without God

Therefore, you can't put God out of your love life, or you have none! You may think you have a love life, but in reality, you can't have a love life without God.

Unfortunately, many Christians love one another more than they love God. Some Christians love their husband, wife, parents or other people more than they love God. But actually their love is defective because they're putting their love priorities in the wrong order. Their love is not working properly because they don't know how to love God first.

To illustrate this principle, let's look again at the story of Martha and Mary in the tenth chapter of Luke.

> **Now it came to pass, as they went, that he entered into a certain village: and a certain woman named Martha received him into her house. And she had a sister called Mary, which also sat at Jesus' feet, and heard his word. But Martha was cumbered about much serving, and came to him, and said, Lord, dost thou not care that my sister hath left me to serve alone? bid her therefore that she help me. And Jesus answered and said unto her, Martha, Martha, thou art careful and**

troubled about many things: But one thing is needful: and Mary hath chosen that good part, which shall not be taken away from her.

Luke 10:38-42

I can imagine that Martha was sincerely trying to use her work and service to demonstrate her love for the Lord. I can imagine she was attempting, as so many of us often do, to show Jesus how much she loved Him through her hard work. But Jesus told her the only thing He wanted was for her to sit at His feet and fellowship with Him as Mary was doing.

Not by Works

Here we see one person loving the Lord by fellowshipping with the Father in His Word, and the other attempting to love Him through work and service. But, child of God, it has never been by your works that God is glorified. God wants the glory for everything that you do anyway. He wants the glory for the fact that you were able to get up this morning. He wants the glory for whatever was wrong last week that's all right now. God wants the glory for your healed body. God wants the glory for your sound mind. God wants the glory for the finances that you do have.

It may be little or much, but He still wants the glory for it. He wants the glory for your deliverance from whatever trouble might happen tomorrow. The Bible says our relationship with God doesn't depend on our works, but on His grace (Ephesians 2:8,9). God doesn't need our work. But He does want us to have a personal, intimate loving relationship with Him.

Getting to Know Him

The importance God places on developing a loving relationship with Him instead of just doing good works in His name is graphically illustrated by something Jesus said in the seventh chapter of Matthew. Warning His disciples about false prophets, He said:

> **Many will say to me in that day, Lord, Lord, have we not prophesied in thy name? and in thy name have cast out devils? and in thy name done *many wonderful works?* And then will I profess unto them, I never *knew* you: depart from me, ye that work iniquity.**

> **MATTHEW 7:22,23**

I want you to underline in your Bible the word *knew* in this passage. Jesus here makes a very important statement which, if we're not careful, we'll overlook. This word *knew* comes from a Greek word *ginosko*[1], which means "to know by experience or effort." It means "the knowledge gained as a result of prolonged practice." What you know, you know through the results of prolonged practice. This word *knew* in the Greek means "knowledge grounded in personal experience," knowledge that has been grounded in or that has been gathered and obtained through personal experience. This knowledge did not come from what you read or from what you've studied — this is the knowledge you have obtained through your own individual personal experience.

As Jesus uses the word *knew,* it simply means "to get to know." So in this verse, when He says, "I never knew you," He means "I never had knowledge of you grounded in personal experience. I never had the time to have prolonged practice with you. Yes, I knew *about* you, but there were certain things that I couldn't gather knowledge about concerning you, because we didn't have practice together. There was no fellowship together. There was nothing I learned about you through the time we spent together."

The people He was talking about were shocked. "But wait a minute, Lord," they said in effect. "I've prophesied in Your name! That's spiritual! Wait a minute, Lord, I've cast out devils! And Lord, I have done many wonderful works!"

Jesus said, "Yes, but the knowledge you obtained, you obtained from memorizing your notes. Or you obtained it from a book you bought just to increase your intellectual knowledge. You even prayed in the mornings just so you could say, 'I prayed in the morning,' but you never even got past the gate. You did many wonderful works, but the knowledge you obtained, you didn't obtain through personal experience with Me."

Wow! That's a pretty harsh statement. Particularly when He followed it up with **depart from me, ye that work iniquity** (v. 23).

Personal Experience with God

You see, child of God, there's something very important we must understand about the fruit of love. The fruit we want to cultivate is love developed in a relationship with our heavenly Father. And the way that love develops is through fellowship with Him in His Word and in prayer. I read the Word because I'm in love with Him. And the times that I spend with Him in prayer, study, and meditation increase my personal knowledge of Him. As I spend time in the Word and in prayer, I get to know Him by personal experience. Then, when someone says something about God I know whether it's right or wrong because of my personal experience with my heavenly Father. I know His nature!

Because I have a personal, intimate, loving relationship with the Father, I know He wasn't responsible for a young child's death in an auto accident. No one can convince me God gave a woman cancer, because I know Him as Healer. I have personal experience with Him as Healer. I know God doesn't have any sickness or disease to give anyone. And I know He's a God of love and grace Who wouldn't do anything to hurt His children.

Sometimes people say things like "Well, you know, maybe it's the will of God that we suffer from this cancer." No! You don't know my Father. You don't know Him; you have not yet *known* my Father! You have an intellectual assimilation of what He may be *about,* but you've never experienced Him.

You know how you can misjudge somebody by having read something about them or by hearing something about them that was taken out of context? Then when you finally got an opportunity to have a personal experience with them, it didn't match what you read? It didn't match what you saw on television. And all of a sudden, you had to repent because now the knowledge you have obtained comes through a personal experience with them.

That's what I mean about spending enough time with God to develop a close, loving relationship with Him as your heavenly Father. When you have a relationship with God grounded in personal experience, what you read in the Word about Him will just be a confirmation of the time that you spent with Him. You will understand what you read because now you know God for yourself.

Therefore, when you hear or read something that is wrong doctrine, you will know it's wrong doctrine because you know what you know about God from your own experience. Even though you don't know all the Scriptures and may not be familiar with the theology behind it, you will know, because you know Him. It will be impossible to convince you to believe something wrong and unscriptural about God because you have *gotten to know* Him personally and intimately through time spent with Him and through prolonged practice.

The Benefits

What are the benefits of reordering our priorities and getting our concept of the fruit of love straightened out? Specifically, how is learning to love God first, myself second and then others going to enable me to trouble my trouble?

Of course, the benefits of learning to love, particularly of learning to love God as my heavenly Father, are incalculable. But since we're talking about overcoming trouble in this book, I'm going to discuss two primary benefits of learning to use the force of love properly:

First, love brings freedom from fear, and second, love enables me to conquer all things.

Benefit No. 1: No Fear in Love

The first benefit of cultivating love for the Father is freedom from fear.

There is no fear in love; but perfect love casteth out fear: because fear hath torment. He that feareth is not made perfect in love.

1 JOHN 4:18

When you develop this love relationship for God, you will begin to walk in a total absence of fear. When you've made loving God your first priority in obedience to Jesus' command in Matthew

22:37, you won't fear what men can do to you. You won't fear what might happen in this circumstance or that situation.

Having a loving relationship with the Father is like being hand-cuffed to God twenty-four hours a day, seven days a week. If you knew God were that near to you at all times, you wouldn't be afraid of anything, would you? Well, the fact is, the Word says God *is* that close to you. He said He will be with you always (Matthew 28:20).

It's when we forget how close the Father is to us that we become fearful. We live in the times Jesus predicted in Luke 21:26, when men's hearts are **failing them for fear,** and we forget that God *knows* the effects of the cancerous fear in our society. For some reason, we assume, or we speculate, that God might not know what's going on here.

And then we pull out the "what if's?" "What if God really does-n't understand how bad it is? I mean, the number one killer in today's society is heart attack! God may not know what's happen-ing!" You may not believe we think like that, but we do. Each and every one of us has thought at one time or another, "Maybe God doesn't know how badly I need this thing here."

Even the Hairs on Your Head

But in Matthew 6:31 and 32, Jesus told us not to worry about having food to eat and something to drink and clothes to wear because, He said:

> **Your heavenly Father knoweth that ye have need of all these things.**
>
> **MATTHEW 6:32**

And you want to reply to your heavenly Father, "Well, if You *knoweth* that I have need of all these things, why don't You *giveth* me these things that I need?"

Actually, there is a reason, child of God. He knows these things, and if you'll hold on now, I'll tell you why you get in those situations sometimes. But let me finish this point here. God *knew* this situation was coming up. He's not so far from you that He doesn't know what's going on with you. "Well, Brother Dollar, if He's not that far from me, why doesn't He do something?"

Well, let's go on a little farther. Jesus says something very interesting about the Father's awareness of us in the tenth chapter of Matthew.

> **Are not two sparrows sold for a farthing? and one of them shall not fall on the ground without your Father. But the very hairs of your head are all numbered. Fear ye not therefore, ye are of more value than many sparrows.**

> **MATTHEW 10:29-31**

Now, I want you to underline the phrase in verse 31, **fear ye not therefore. Fear ye not *therefore*.** Look at the word *therefore*. *Therefore,* what? *Therefore* that God knows the number of hairs on your head. How will the fact that God knows the number of hairs on my head help me not to fear? What is Jesus really telling me here? What was He saying to the disciples? He was telling them that if they would develop a relationship with God, to the point of fully realizing their loving Father's infinite awareness of them, they would no longer fear.

Why?

Because they would then realize how aware of them God is.

God is saying, "I am so aware of you, I know the number of hairs on your head!" And zero is a number, so if you don't have any, God knows it! If you've added some, God knows it! If you've lost some, God knows it! He knew when you lost it, He knew when you added it, and He knew what it was the day you were born in this earth! What is He saying? He's saying, "I have always, and I am still, and I always will be infinitely aware of you!"

How much awareness? So aware of you — here's the detail — so aware of you that every hair on your head is numbered. That's pretty aware, isn't it? You know how detailed it is to sit there and count each hair? That's how aware He is of you.

Don't tell me He's not there! Don't tell me He is way out in the cosmos somewhere! Don't tell me He's in the distant heavens, and isn't aware that you need a car. That He's not aware that you need a job. That He is not aware that you need help. God is aware!

"Well, Brother Dollar, I hear what you're saying, *but....*" There you go with that "but" again! "If He's that aware of my situation and circumstance, then why doesn't He do something? I'm going down for the third time here. Why doesn't God do something?"

It's Your Decision

Child of God, why don't *you* do something? I've heard people say what they don't have to do and what they don't want to do. And I have finally come to the point of agreeing — you *don't have* to tithe, you *don't have* to live holy, you *don't have* to go to church ever again. You don't have to read your Bible. You don't have to pray in the Spirit. In fact, you don't have to pray at all. You don't have to praise God. You're absolutely right — you don't have to do anything except die someday. That's about all you have to do. But everything else — you absolutely don't have to do it.

You can make your decision not to tithe — but don't question God why you don't have a job and why your car keeps breaking down, you can't pay your bills, and everything in your house is falling apart.

You can make a decision not to read the Word, but don't question God why you're depressed and distressed and feeling lonely all the time.

You can make a decision not to live holy, but don't go to God and ask Him why your life is a living hell — because He said, **I have set before you life and death, blessing and cursing: there-fore** *choose...* (Deuteronomy 30:19). God said, "*You* choose."

The Default Setting

So, you're right, you don't have to do anything. You don't even have to make a choice. But if you don't deliberately choose life and blessing, you'll get death and cursing by default. God has given us a choice, and He even told us which choice to make.

...Therefore *choose life,* **that both thou and thy seed may live.**

DEUTERONOMY 30:19

God wants you to choose life. He won't force you to. But if you don't choose life, you're automatically choosing death. The "default setting" in this natural world is the law of sin and death. If you don't choose blessing and then get in the Word and find out what it says about receiving the blessings and benefits of salvation, don't blame God if the curse manifests itself in your life. Don't wonder why you're always in trouble, when you haven't done the things the Bible says you must do to overcome it.

And don't look at me and say, "I wonder why he doesn't seem to have any trouble?" Who says I don't have trouble? Sure, the devil brings trouble against me, but I don't have to let it trouble me for one simple reason — *I have chosen.* I'm the man of my house, and I have chosen that **as for me and my house, we will serve the Lord** (Joshua 24:15).

I have chosen that as for me and my house, we're going to tithe; we're going to confess His Word; we're going to study His Word; we're going to live a holy life. We've made our decision.

Now, what does that decision do? It says to God, "You have free access, freedom, and my permission, to come in and bring Your Word to pass in my life and the life of my family."

The answer to the complaint "if God is aware of my situation, why doesn't He do something for me?" is — *because you won't do something for yourself!* You haven't done the needful part. You haven't made the choice that allows Him to come in and do something for you. And until you make the choice that allows God to come in and do something for you, God will be very aware of your circumstance and situation, but He won't be able to do anything about it.

For example, the municipal government of a city may be aware of its needs for street repairs, more parks, and better schools in their community. But there are only certain things they can do to solve these problems until they hold a bond election and get permission from the voters to spend the money. The people on the city council and the school board may be good people who are trying to do good things for the citizens of the city. But they can't solve the city's problems without the proper permission from the voters. That's the way our system of government works.

If You Could Only See the Movie

God is the same way. He set up the system we've been calling the "Word system" which says that if you do not give Him permission and allow Him access into your situations and circumstances, then there's only so much He can do.

Now the "so much" that He does do is called *mercy*. If you only knew the bigger mess you would be in by not allowing Him to come in with His loving-kindness, mercy, and grace.... You may think it's bad now, but it's nowhere near as bad as what it could be. God loves you so much that He can't stand to see you continue in deception and continue to think you know more than He knows. He can't stand to see that. So every now and then, He just sort of slips His little finger in here and there and helps you out even though you haven't really given Him permission. And because of His mercy, your situation is not as bad as it *could* have been!

If God could show you a movie of how much worse your situation *could* have turned out, you would recognize that single set of footprints on the sand behind you as God's. You would *know* it was God Who was carrying you through that situation.

So we must come to the place of recognizing that we have to make choices. That's what life is — it's a lot of choices. We are all products of decisions and choices. But you yourself have to make those choices. Nobody, including God, can make them for you. And if God can't do it, what makes you think man can? God can't — God *won't* — make you do what you don't decide to do. He won't do it. He absolutely refuses to do so.

But He is still aware. God is there. His mercy and His forgiveness endure forever. Goodness and mercy shall follow you all the days of your life (Psalm 23:6). God is there. He's with you always. He's concerned about you. He's aware of you. But there are certain decisions you have to make for yourself.

Handcuffed to God

We know God is with us everywhere no matter what trouble we get ourselves into, because He promised He would be. The Bible says:

> **Let your conversation be without covetousness; and be content with such things as ye have: for he hath said, I will never leave thee, nor forsake thee.**
>
> **So that we may boldly say, The Lord is my helper, and I will not fear what man shall do unto me.**
>
> **HEBREWS 13:5,6**

Notice this Scripture says that God said one thing, *so* we can say another thing. He said, **I will never leave thee, nor forsake thee** so that *we* can say, **The Lord is my helper, and I will not fear what man shall do unto me.** I can say, "The Lord is my helper, and I will not fear what man can do to me," only because *He* said, "I will never leave you nor forsake you." Therefore, now I'm like a man handcuffed to God. Since He will never leave me nor forsake me, what am I to fear? What am I afraid of? God is on my side.

How can I be sure? I'm sure because I've developed a loving relationship with my heavenly Father. Like Moses, I'm not afraid even in fearful situations because **by faith** I endure **as seeing him who is invisible** (Hebrews 11:27).

Now, how do I see what's invisible? Let me give an example. Suppose I have a friend, or somebody that I really trust, and they're always on time, their word is good, their integrity is good. When they tell me something, I know it's just as good as gold. Do I have to see it? No. My knowledge gained and grounded in personal relationship has given me all I need to know. I know that individual will produce what they say. I know from long personal experience with that person that their word is good.

And so it is in my relationship with God. Based on what was grounded in personal experience, I begin to see something that's invisible. By knowledge that I gained through prolonged practice with God, I can be absolutely sure that God will do what He said He will do. I can come on out of my situation just as Moses did, seeing Him who is invisible.

And how do I see Him who is invisible? I see Him through His Word, through His promises. And because I know Him through personal experience, I am fully persuaded that what He promised, He will do. I'm no longer afraid because I've perfected and matured my love for God and **perfect love casteth out fear** (1 John 4:18).

Benefit No. 2: Love Conquers All Things

The second benefit of developing the fruit of love towards the Father is that it enables a person to conquer all things. Remember, it is towards *God* that I must get this love relationship right. When I make loving God my priority, that relationship with the Father enables me to conquer all things. And if I can get into position to conquer all things, I certainly should be able to overcome trouble! Let's see why having a loving relationship with my heavenly Father will enable me to overcome trouble.

Failure Proof

First of all, 1 Corinthians 13:8 says **Love never fails** (NIV). Now, why will love never fail? What is it about love that's so powerful? What is it about love that produces such great and guaranteed results? How is it that Paul could be so bold and have such audacity as to declare that love *never* fails?

First John 4 gives us an answer to that question.

> **...Every one that loveth is born of God, and knoweth God.**
>
> **He that loveth not knoweth not God; for God is love.**
>
> 1 JOHN 4:7,8

Now put these two Scriptures together. **For God is love** and **love never fails.** So I would be correct in saying: God never fails, because God is love. Therefore, if you'll begin to operate in love, you'll begin to duplicate God. And when you duplicate God, the devil won't be able to tell the difference between Him and you. When you're laying hands on the sick, you duplicate God. When you're speaking in tongues, you duplicate God.

And when you put on love and begin operating in love right in the midst of the temptation not to do so, then you are God's identical twin. When you are imitating God by putting on love, somebody will look at you and say, "I know this person comes from the Tribe of Judah. They must be kin to that Jehovah fellow — because they look just like Him!"

And that's what we have failed to remember in our walk as Christians. We've failed to remember that all our revelation knowledge, all our gifts of the Spirit, all our speaking in tongues and dynamic understanding of prayer — means absolutely nothing if a Christian is not clothed in love. You're not a witness, neither can you be a good witness without clothing yourself in love. If you haven't put on love, people will forget about your demonstration of power because it will be completely erased when they see what kind of character you have.

Putting His Anointing On

Love never fails. Absolutely never fails. Why? Because God never fails. When you put love on, you put God on. And when you put God on, you put His life, His *zoe,* His power, His anointing on.

You can't help but increase when you put love on. Many Christians aren't increasing in their spiritual lives because they won't put love on. They're anointed in one area, but they're missing out in another area. They mistakenly think their anointing for one area will carry over into other areas. But, child of God, your anointing in one area won't make you successful in other areas.

However, there *is* something you can do that guarantees you *any* anointing to accomplish anything you need to accomplish, and *that is* — putting on love. The love of God is the power that turns on joy. It's the power that turns on peace. It's the power that turns on longsuffering. It's the power that turns on faith. It *is* anointed. When I put love on, I put God on. When I put God on, I put on His Anointed One *and* His Anointing.

When you put love on, you put God on, and you can't fail because God is love and He can't fail. Anointing is no problem when you operate in love.

Getting your bills paid is no problem when you're operating in love. Getting healed is no problem when you operate in love. Troubling your trouble is no problem when you operate in love.

When you get God on you, you get the anointing on you, and you then have the ability to do whatever you need to do to get the victory.

Loving God with all your heart and all your soul and all your mind, and getting to know your heavenly Father intimately by personal experience will make you more than a conqueror. When you realize how deeply God loves you and how close He always is to you, you'll never fear trouble again. After all, what trouble could separate you from the love of God?

> **Who shall separate us from the love of Christ? shall tribulation, or distress, or persecution, or famine, or nakedness, or peril, or sword?**
>
> **As it is written, For thy sake we are killed all the day long; we are accounted as sheep for the slaughter.**
>
> **Nay, in all these things we are more than conquerors through him that loved us.**
>
> **For I am persuaded, that neither death, nor life, nor angels, nor principalities, nor powers, nor things present, nor things to come,**
>
> **Nor height, nor depth, nor any other creature, shall be able to separate us from the love of God, which is in Christ Jesus our Lord.**
>
> ROMANS 8:35-39

In the next chapter, we're going to learn how cultivating a loving relationship with our heavenly Father will help us overcome trouble in our relationships with other people. If we're to be more than conquerors, walk free from fear, and trouble our trouble every time it shows up, we must know how to love God. It's only as we truly learn to know and love God that we can learn to love ourselves and then to love our neighbors as ourselves.

Right now, make a decision to put on the fruit of love. Say the following prayer aloud:

Heavenly Father, right now, in the name of Jesus, I make a decision to develop a relationship with You, a relationship in which I will have knowledge of You grounded in personal experience. Father, I decide now to clothe my life in love. I decide now to love You, then to love myself, so that I can love others. Father, give me a revelation, a working revelation, of Your love, so as I begin to walk in love, I, too, will see victory in every area of my life. In Jesus' Name. Amen.

[1] W.E. Vine, "An Expository Dictionary of New Testament Words," *Vine's Compete Expository Dictionary of Old and New Testament Words,* (Nashville: Thomas Nelson Publishers, 1985), p. 346.

7

Troubling Your Trouble
With the Force of Love

Part 2: Loving God and Loving Others

I said in the last chapter that if we are to be able to trouble our trouble with the force of love, we must get our priorities right in our love life. Jesus told us that the proper order of love is to love our heavenly Father first before we try to love anyone else. And we have to learn to love ourselves before we can love our neighbors. Therefore, it's vitally important that we learn to love the Father. We must cultivate and develop a loving relationship with God before our other love relationships will work properly.

Probably the greatest and the most painful kind of trouble any of us experience is trouble in relationships. And one of the reasons we have trouble in our relationships with our families and friends is that we try to carry on these relationships without having a love relationship with God. We try to operate in the system of love which God designed, but we dump God out of the system.

The system won't work properly without a relationship with God because God is the battery for the system. God is what makes the system work.

If I'm going to love you correctly, then I'd better understand the love towards the Father.

If I'm going to love myself correctly, then I'd better understand the love towards the Father.

If you husbands want to love your wives correctly, then you'd better understand the love towards the Father.

If you wives are to love your husbands correctly, then you'd better understand the love towards the Father.

If you try to carry on this love relationship, which God created, if you try to carry on this love system, which God represents, without Him, it won't work. Because the system will not work without the power source that runs it. And that power source is God.

You Must Cultivate the Fruit of Love

In this chapter, we are going to talk first about cultivating the fruit of love towards our heavenly Father. Then we'll look at how developing a proper vertical relationship with God enables us to walk in love in our horizontal relationships with others.

Trouble in our horizontal relationships can only be overcome by a proper vertical relationship with our heavenly Father. So before we can love others properly, we must first cultivate our love for God. Now, when you hear the word *cultivate,* I'd like you to realize that it is you who will have to do something to make this thing come to pass. It is not something that you can pray and hope about and then wake up one day and find it is there. It is something you have to cultivate and deliberately work to develop. *To cultivate* something means that you must work at it and work it.

For instance, if I want to pick collard greens out of my backyard, I have to do more than say, "Oh, dear God, I want some collard greens; please let 'em be in the backyard." No. I have to plant; I have to water; I have to cultivate. I have to keep the weeds out and do what's necessary to earn that harvest of collard greens. When I've done all that's required to develop those plants, *then* I can eat the fruit of my labor. I can enjoy a mess of collard greens with my cornbread because I cultivated my garden and worked to bring in a harvest.

And in the same way, we must actively cultivate the fruit of love towards the heavenly Father. Remember, we're talking about cultivating and developing love *towards the heavenly Father first.* If we can develop a right vertical relationship with our Father in heaven, then we will establish simultaneously right horizontal relationships here on earth. In other words, if we can develop the correct relationship between man and God, then we will have no problem establishing correct relationships between man and man.

Our problem has been that we've tried to carry on horizontal relationships with other people without first establishing the vertical relationship with God. And that won't work. It won't work because God is love, and the system won't work without Him. It's only as we learn to love God with the kind of love the Bible describes in 1 Corinthians 13 that we'll be able to apply this kind of love to our relationships with ourselves and with other people. It's only as we learn to love God that we become able to love ourselves and others.

What's in It for Me?

"But, Brother Dollar," I hear you say, "All this cultivating and developing sounds like a lot of hard work. My relationships with people seem to be going along all right. Exactly how is cultivating this vertical relationship with God going to benefit me? Why should I love God anyway? And how will loving God really help me when I have trouble loving somebody else?"

Well, hang on a minute, and I'll show you. I'm going to show you how Jesus Himself used His vertical relationship with His heavenly Father to overcome a time of trouble and temptation in His earthly family relationships. But first we need to lay a foundation.

First of all, let's look at the question of why you should have a personal relationship with God. Why should you do all the work of developing and cultivating the fruit of love for a Person you can't even see? It's a common question.

You can try to witness to certain people to get born again, and you'll say, "Jesus loves you. God loves you." But they say, "What has God ever done for me? If He loves me, then why am I in the mess I'm in right now? If He loves me, then why am I going through what I'm going through? God doesn't love me. Where is His love? How can you say God loves me?"

That's why it took me such a long time to get born again. The only reason I didn't get born again sooner was that I didn't know why I should love God. The only reason I could see was that people talked about it, and they went to church. But it was just a religious practice to me. I saw no reason to get born again. I couldn't see where God did anything as far as I was personally concerned.

Why Should I Love God?

The Book of Ephesians gives us one of the reasons why we should love God and why we should walk in love with one another.

> **Be ye therefore followers of God, as dear children;**
>
> **And walk in love, as Christ also hath loved us, and hath given himself for us an offering and a sacrifice to God for sweet-smelling savour.**
>
> **EPHESIANS 5:1,2**

The Amplified Bible translates that same passage this way:

Therefore be imitators of God [copy Him and follow His example], as well-beloved children [imitate their father].

And walk in love, [esteeming and delighting in one another] as Christ loved us and gave Himself up for us, a slain offering and sacrifice to God [for you, so that it may become] a sweet fragrance.

EPHESIANS 5:1,2,AMP

Now, I see why I should love God — He died for me. He died for me before I was even formed into a thought. That's staggering. When I didn't even exist, He made a decision to die for me. Jesus died for me before I was formed into a thought.

He died for me. He died for you. Why would He die for you and for me? Because He loved us. And because He loved us, He gave His life, He shed His blood. That whipping with the cat-o-nine tails was for you and me. We were not even born, but He was whipped for you and for me. Glory to God. Climbing up Calvary's hill with that big cross on His back was for you and me. When He let the nails go in, it was for you and for me. And remember, He had to allow it. No man could take His life; He had to give it up. He could have called legions of angels to rescue Him, but He loved us so much He died on the Cross for you and for me.

On the cross He became every sickness and disease. He became cancer; He became the common cold; He became the flu; He became diabetes; He became leukemia; He became AIDS; He became depression; He became distress. Every evil that exists, He became. Why? Because He loved us.

He took your place, and He went to hell on your behalf. He was in love with you, and He went to hell so you don't have to go. He spent three days and three nights in hell so you won't have to spend one day or one night there. And His love didn't stop there. On the third day, He rose from the dead to make sure that you received everything He had left you.

Why?

Because He was in love with you.

You have to understand — Love went to the cross. Love was crucified, dead and buried. Love went to hell for three days and three nights. Love got up from the grave on the third day. Love sat down on the right hand of God the Father Almighty.

Love is interceding for you and me right now. Love is standing between us and the Father and saying to Him, "Don't look at them like they used to look, Father. Don't see them as unworthy anymore. Don't see them as filthy rags anymore. Don't see them as hell-bound any more. Father, look at them through Me and see them as righteous. Look at them through Me and see them as worthy."

Jesus knows that Satan is accusing the brethren. And He's sitting there because He loves you, saying, "No, Father, they're fine. No, Father, they're with me. Father, I know they've sinned, but My blood is there and it will cleanse them of all of their sin."

It's Not Over Yet!

Love. Love. Love died for us. And do you know what? Love is coming back again. The relationship is not over yet. He loves us so much He told us:

In my Father's house are many mansions: if it were not so, I would have told you. I go to prepare a place for you.

And if I go and prepare a place for you, I will come again, and receive you unto myself; that where I am, there ye may be also.

JOHN 14:2,3

Jesus said, "I'm going to come back and get you. And whether you're dead or alive when I come back, I've got a new outfit for you. If you are dead, then the dead in Christ shall rise first, and they shall take off corruption and put on incorruption. If you're alive when I come, then you're going to take off your mortal flesh and slip into a flesh of immortality. But when you both see me and meet me in the air, you're going to see Love, and you're going look just like me."

Love. Love. Love is coming back!

Now let me ask you a question. How can you not love a man like that? He gave you His name. He gave you His authority. He gave you His Spirit. He gave you a way to get His mind. He's given you everything that pertains to life and godliness. He's given you angels to watch over you, to command, to send forth. He's given you the power to bind and to loose. He's given you all that heaven has. He's prepared a table before you in the presence of your enemies. He's given you His Word.

What *else* can He do for you? What *else?* He's given you His life. *What else* can He do for you? *What else* can He do? He's given you everything that He has. And He said "I made you to sit with Me in heavenly places."

Here you are, trying to get to heaven, and you haven't even recognized that He's already made you to sit with Him in heavenly places (Ephesians 1:3,20). Because if you can go to heaven, if you're good enough to go to heaven, then you're good enough to have a little heaven on the inside of you right now while you're here on earth. Glory to God!

How can you not love a man like this? See, that's the gospel. That's the good news. That's the good news that if you're poor, Jesus is anointed to deliver you from poverty. If you have blinded eyes, Jesus can open up your blinded eyes.

Oh, yes, my sight has now been developed. He did all that for me? Yes. Somebody says, "I thought He did it all for the Christians." No. Paul says in Romans 5:

While we were yet sinners, Christ died for us.

ROMANS 5:8

Christ died for you before you knew Him. So how can you not love Him? The only answer I can come up with is you just don't know what He did for you. Yes, He did all that just for you. How could you not love Him?

Such an Insult

Now can you see why it's such an insult to your heavenly Father when you love your addictions and your habits more than you love God? Can you see what an insult it is when you love your local professional sports team more than you love God? As good as some of those men may be, they didn't die for you. Those professional football players didn't go to hell for you. Those baseball players didn't get up on the third day on your behalf. Yet, you give them all the hand claps they want. You give them all the praise they want. You give them all the money they want.

Yet, look at what Jesus did for you. And we still can't get you to clap on Sunday mornings. You won't lift your hands up in praise to God. If we ask you to shout, you think, "I'm not supposed to shout in church."

And oh, don't even think about asking you for your money! Yet, you'll go and pay fifteen or twenty dollars for a ticket to a game which will last three or four hours and be forgotten the next day. You'll spend all that money at the game but then complain about giving money to the Man Who purchased your ticket to heaven with His own blood and didn't charge you a dime for it. How can you not love a man like this?

Why should we love God and cultivate an intimate relationship with Him? Because He died for us and made it possible for us to be born again.

Spending Time With the Father

"Well, Brother Dollar, you've convinced me I should make the effort to cultivate a loving relationship with my heavenly Father," you say. "But how do I do that? Exactly where do I start in getting to know Him?"

Start where you would start in getting to know anyone — start spending time with Him. Start talking with Him and listening to Him. Start watching what He does, and then start imitating and copying Him. That's what Jesus did. Jesus said He didn't do anything He hadn't seen the Father do.

But Jesus answered them, My Father worketh hitherto, and I work....Verily, verily, I say unto you, The Son can do

nothing of himself, but what he seeth the Father do: for what things soever he doeth, these also doeth the Son likewise.

JOHN 5:17,19

Do you remember the Scripture (John 15:5) which says that without the Lord you can do nothing? Are you aware that you can't do anything without the Lord? We forget that too often.

You see, we've been deceived by this world's system into thinking that success can be gained without God. But the world is wrong. And unfortunately, it usually takes your getting to the end of your rope to find out there's no success without Him. All the money in the world is nothing without God. All the prestige and the titles in the world are nothing without God. They can crown you prince of the earth, but it will be nothing without God.

You can't do anything without God. Even Jesus admitted that the Son could do nothing of Himself. Jesus gave the credit to the Father for everything He did. He said He could do nothing *but* what He saw the Father do. So since the Bible says we are to be imitators of God, we should also do what the Father does.

How are you and I going to see what the Father does? *The only way I can see what the Father does is through His Word. I will see the Father and get to know Him by spending time in His Word.* That's the only way I can see what the Father does.

The Son can do nothing of himself, but what he seeth the Father do.

JOHN 5:19

Likewise, we cannot walk in love without spending time with the Father.

Why We're Flunking

How can you expect to walk in love the way the Father does without spending enough time with Him to find out how He walks in love? People are flunking the love walk because they've been trying to operate in love without having ever spent enough time with the Father to find out how to walk in love. You can't walk in love without finding out how the Father walks in love. That's why you don't know how to love your husband. And that's why you don't know how to love your wife. That's why you don't know how to love one another. That's why you justify being mad at somebody for years — because you haven't seen or known how the Father loves. Therefore, you have nothing to imitate.

There is something wrong with the vertical relationship. That's why we're flunking the horizontal relationships. If you want to fix the horizontal relationship — that is, your relationships with everybody and everything else — your vertical relationship with God must first be in working order. To fix the horizontal relationships, we must make an adjustment in our vertical relationship. Once we have adjusted our vertical relationship, then we'll know how to deal with everybody on this horizontal plane.

Our problem is we've tried to live totally on a horizontal plane while ignoring the vertical plane. And when you ignore your vertical relationship with God, your horizontal relationships will be missing the essential ingredient that they need to work.

As we've said, any system needs a power source, and the only power source for the love system is the love of God. The only way you can get the power you need to walk in love in your relationships with other people is to cultivate the fruit of love with your heavenly Father.

Hooking Up the Power

The Bible says God is the *only source* of the power we need to operate in the love walk.

Beloved, let us love one another: for love is of God; and every one that loveth is born of God, and knoweth God.

He that loveth not knoweth not God; for God is love.

1 JOHN 4:7,8

He that loveth not knoweth not God.... That ought to be plain enough. There's no way you can operate in love without knowing God. You'll never know how to love, particularly to love the unlovable and to love in situations where it's difficult to walk in love, without knowing God. It's humanly impossible to love some people and to walk in love in some situations unless you're loving with the love of God. It's *humanly impossible*. That's why you have to hook up with Somebody Who's above the human. You can't do it in your natural strength. You have to hook up with the *super* of God to do it.

The Secret Rewards

It's only as we know God that we know how to love one another. It's your relationship with your heavenly Father that you cultivate by spending time with Him that will give you the power and the anointing you need to walk in love. It never ceases to amaze me how concerned Christians are about what they can produce in front of the public. But it is not what you do in public that produces great rewards. It is what you do in secret that produces great rewards.

I may not hear your prayers when you're by yourself alone with God. But I will see openly the result of your time spent with God in His anointing.

It disturbs me when I hear great singers and choral groups and hear great preachers in the pulpit who appear to have a dynamic love relationship with God. On the basis of their singing and preaching and their demonstration of power on the platform, you would swear that these men and women really love the Lord. And yet, when you get together with them after they get off the stage — and that's what it should be called because it's become a place of performance rather than a place of personal relationship and conviction — you hear the way they talk and see how they act, your heart drops. You're heartbroken because you thought they were really in love with God, but now you see that they don't even know Him.

They don't even know Him. And it's sad because tradition has deceived them into thinking that it is when I show my greatness in the pulpit or in front of the public that they'll know I love God. And God will bless me. No, no, no. You've got it backwards. *It is what you do behind closed doors, it is what you do in the secret place alone with the Father that witnesses to the quality of your relationship with God.*

You may love to lift your hands in public, but do you lift them when you're in your secret place? You may be the loudest one in corporate prayer, but do you pray like that when in your secret place? You love to sing your solo every chance you get, but do you sing to the Lord in your secret place? You see, these things have not been designed for public auditions. They are things that should be used in the secret place, to minister to and fellowship with the Lord. You must cultivate your love for Him so that when you come out of the secret place, everybody who comes in contact with the anointing that's on your life will know that you spent quality time with God.

It's what you do in secret when nobody's looking that will be visible on your life when you get up in public. It's what you do in secret, fellowshipping with Him in your secret place, that God says He will reward you openly for (Matthew 6:1-6).

Child of God, if you want to be effective in the kingdom of God, you must spend time developing a vertical relationship with the heavenly Father. That's the only way you will be effective in your horizontal relationships with other people. When times of tempting and trouble come in your relationships with others, the *only way* you can keep from failing in your love walk is to have available a reservoir of time spent alone with the Father. It's in that time alone with Him that you cultivate the fruit of love you can draw on to get you through the rough times.

Jesus Overcame Trouble with the Fruit of Love

Even Jesus had an experience in which He might have failed in love if He had not had that vertical relationship with God to keep Him steady. Jesus had to depend on His vertical relationship with His Father in times of great temptation in order to adjust His horizontal relationship with other people. And when He did that, the anointing of God came on Him, and He was able to do miracles.

One of the times of greatest testing in Jesus' life came when He learned that his cousin John [the Baptist] had been killed by Herod the Tetrarch. We find the story in Matthew 14.

At that time Herod the tetrarch heard of the fame of Jesus,
And said unto his servants, This is John the Baptist; he is

risen from the dead; and therefore mighty works do shew forth themselves in him. For Herod had laid hold on John, and bound him, and put him in prison for Herodias' sake, his brother Philip's wife. For John said unto him, It is not lawful for thee to have her. And when he would have put him to death, he feared the multitude, because they counted him as a prophet. But when Herod's birthday was kept, the daughter of Herodias danced before them, and pleased Herod. Whereupon he promised with an oath to give her whatsoever she would ask. And she, being before instructed of her mother, said, Give me here John Baptist's head in a charger. And the king was sorry: nevertheless for the oath's sake, and them which sat with him at meat, he commanded it to be given her. And he sent, and beheaded John in the prison. And his head was brought in a charger, and given to the damsel; and she brought it to her mother. And his disciples came, and took up the body, and buried it, and went and told Jesus [the first cousin of John].

MATTHEW 14:1-12

Put Yourself in His Shoes

Now I want you to put yourself in the shoes of Jesus. His first cousin had been beheaded, and He heard that they were parading his head around in front of Herod's court. That's enough to make you want to cuss, isn't it? You want to do something for revenge, don't you? Your flesh is tempted, isn't it?

Remember, this was Jesus' kin. This was a close relative He had grown up with. Do you remember how when some of you were in school with your brothers or cousins, your mama told you, "He better not get beat up. If he gets beat up, you better get beat up too because if he comes home beat up and you're not beat up, I'm gonna beat you up"? That's what my daddy used to tell me. "Your sisters better not ever come home hurt and you're not hurt." And my sisters would get told, "If he comes home hurt, all you all better be hurt." I'm sure Jesus felt just as angry when He saw any of His brothers, sisters or cousins getting bullied on the school ground as you or I would. I'm sure He wanted to wade into the fight just like you would or I would. After all, He was the oldest, and He probably felt like He ought to look out for the younger kids in the family. Now before you get upset with me, remember that the book of Hebrews says Jesus was *in all points* **tempted like as we are** (Hebrews 4:15). Any sin you or I are tempted to commit, Jesus was tempted to commit.

So how do you think He felt when John's disciples came and told him what had been done to his cousin? John was special to Jesus because he was the only member of His family who really understood Him, who really knew who He was and what He was here on earth to do.

John had baptized Jesus. If anybody understood Jesus' mission, John did. Everybody else in His family kind of thought Jesus was going crazy in the latter part of His ministry, including Mary, His mother. They wanted to cast him off the cliff after He preached in His home church. But John understood Him. John was like a brother to Him.

So Jesus must have been terribly upset when He was told that John had been brutally murdered. I'm convinced He was tempted to lash out in revenge. He may even have wanted to call angels to destroy Herod and everybody connected with him. He was under terrible temptation.

But look what He did.

When Jesus heard of it, he departed thence by ship into a desert place apart.

MATTHEW 14:13

Now here's the revelation I want you to get. *Jesus departed from the horizontal line.* He departed from the horizontal relationships and sought the vertical relationship He had with His heavenly Father. Jesus went off alone to pray and spend time with the Father so that He wouldn't fall into the sin of responding the way His flesh wanted to respond in His horizontal relationships with all the people. He went to get the power of the love of God to keep Him from failing in His love walk. And don't think He couldn't have failed.

[He] **was in all points tempted like as we are, yet without sin.**

HEBREWS 4:15

Jesus could have sinned, but thank God, He didn't.

...And when the people had heard [that Jesus had departed into a desert place apart]**, they followed him on foot out of the cities.**

And Jesus went forth, and saw a great multitude, and was moved with compassion toward them, and he healed their sick.

MATTHEW 14:13,14

And Jesus went forth.... Where did He go forth from? From the vertical line, from time alone in His vertical relationship of fellowship with the Father.

And Jesus...saw a great multitude, and was moved with compassion toward them.

MATTHEW 14:14

Now instead of being moved with distress and anger over the death of John, Jesus was **moved with *compassion*** for the people who had followed Him. Where did He get that compassion? From His relationship with the Father. And what He got from His vertical relationship Jesus was then able to apply to His horizontal relationship with the people. As soon as He began operating in the love of God, the anointing came upon Him.

And he healed their sick.

MATTHEW 14:14

Listen to me, child of God. When it gets rough, when you can't figure it out, and you don't know where you're going to go and how you're going to end up there, go to God. Get yourself filled with God, relate with God, love on God. Straighten out your vertical relationship with the heavenly Father, and He will show you how to relate horizontally.

A River for Everyone

And when you relate horizontally because of what you did by yourself with God in the secret place, *then* you will see something openly. Everybody will benefit from the rivers that come out of your belly. The Bible says that out of our bellies shall flow rivers of living water (John 8:38). What's the difference between a river and a well? A well is just for you — but a river is for everybody. Thank the Lord!

When everything in your relationships with people is messed up and in trouble, when you're having trouble loving lovable people — to say nothing of unlovable ones — do what Jesus did when He had the same problem. Separate yourself from the horizontal plane and seek the vertical relationship with your heavenly Father. Spend time alone with God and let His love adjust your love life. Then you'll be able to walk in the love of God, and you won't fail because love never fails.

Section II:
Walking in the Confidence
of God in Troubled Times

Section II:
Walking in the Confidence of God in Troubled Times

INTRODUCTION:
LIVING IN THE OVERFLOW

In the first section of this book, we emphasized that just because trouble comes, it doesn't have to overcome. Although Jesus told us in John 16:33 that in the world we will have tribulation and trouble, we can have peace and be of good cheer because He has overcome the world. And if Jesus has overcome the world, then we, as born-again believers and heirs of salvation, can overcome it too. If we take our position as joint heirs with Christ and learn to use the weapons He has left us, we can trouble our trouble and overcome it.

However, as I'm sure you've found out (if you've been diligent to apply what I've been teaching you), it's a whole lot easier to study about troubling your trouble than it is to do it! *And it's a whole lot easier to get a one-time victory over some specific area of trouble in your life than it is to keep that victory so trouble doesn't come back in a few days or months.* Satan is a tenacious and persistent foe. He's desperate to steal our peace and to steal the Word of God out of our hearts. He's always looking for an opportunity to drag us right back into the same old mess we've just come out of.

In One Blast

I found that out from personal experience early in my ministry. I discovered that although I was constantly studying and teaching and preaching the Word, something was disturbing my peace. Although I was spending so much time in the Word, preparing sermons and ministering, I was troubled. I began to notice that certain reports would get to me, and they would stay in my spirit and bother me. I knew I felt a little drained every time I finished preaching and ministering the Word. But I thought it was just normal fatigue and that a good night's sleep would take care of it. But I'd go to bed and be unable to sleep because my peace wouldn't come back.

And I found that things which normally would not have bothered me started absolutely nagging the life out of me to the point that I found myself just trying to keep from going under. I'd pray, "Oh, God, what's wrong? Why can't I handle this? Why is this thing affecting me like this, Lord? I should be able to handle this. After all, I handled it last year — why can't I handle it now?"

Finally, I got so depressed I said to God, "I don't feel like I can take this anymore. I'm tired of this. I don't want this anymore. I...I quit. I can't take this." I was in such great distress I felt like I was dying inside, like I was crumbling away. I didn't know what to do to fight the problem because I didn't understand what was wrong.

But the Lord finally got my attention and showed me what was happening. He said, "Son, when these troubles came to you before, they found no room to occupy because you were filled with My Word. But as you continue to pour out in preaching, teaching and ministering, you're forgetting to pour in. You're forgetting to replenish what you've poured out. And when you poured it out and did not pour anything back in, you left that space unoccupied. And that's just what the devil has been waiting for. He's been waiting for some unoccupied space so he can come in and occupy your thinking with bad reports, occupy your thinking with fear, occupy your thinking with worry. *You don't have the ability in the natural to combat these things.* That's why I've given you My Word as a shield to quench the fiery darts of the wicked one."

"What do You mean, Lord?" I asked.

He said, "Any time there is available space, Satan will take it."

And I finally began to understand what He meant. I had been down so far, I didn't want to live anymore. I had been trying to figure out where this deep depression was coming from. Then suddenly, I saw that Satan had been trying to get a foothold in me for months and even years.

The devil's not stupid! When he finally gets a chance to get into a born again Christian who's been giving him a headache for years, do you think he's going to come in lightly? Not hardly! He's going to come in with his heavy artillery. He'll bring in everything he can possibly squeeze in at one time and attempt to wipe you out in one blast!

An Ounce of Prevention

"All right, God," I said, "I see this is my fault. I see where I messed up. I see what happened. Now, please tell me what to do so we can correct the situation and prevent it from happening again."

Well, what the Lord showed me is nothing all that spectacular; it won't make you do flips or dance in the street when you read it. But, child of God, believe me, *it works!*

God showed me that if you wanted to remove something that had been put in a container of water, the best way to remove it is to *create an overflow.* He said to me, "Get in the Word until it creates an overflow."

He told me to get into the Word of God, to start praying the Word of God, start confessing the Word of God three times a day.

Start saying it, start meditating in it, until your heart not only gets filled with it, but begins to overflow. When the overflow begins, whatever was able to get into your heart through your ear-gate or your eye-gate will be washed out by the current of that flow.

The current of the overflow will move the junk out, and only that which is pure, only that which is holy, only that which is of good report will continue to stay within the circulation of the overflow.

"Well, Lord," I said, "what do I do with the overflow?" He said, "Live there. Live in the overflow."

Where Did the Trouble Go?

Now, why should I live in the overflow? I must live in the overflow and minister out of the overflow, because I want to make sure that the material that's occupying the position of my spirit — all the things Paul listed in Philippians 4:8 — doesn't get used up.

I don't want to run dry. When I fill myself with the Word to the point of overflowing, I have a way to prevent junk from the world and the devil from getting in. When I live in the overflow, I also have a way to move out into the things of God. I now have enough Word occupying the space in my heart to leave no room for Satan. *And,* I have enough left over to minister to others without being constantly depleted myself.

Child of God, I want to tell you — when you get yourself filled to overflowing with the Word, all of a sudden you'll wonder what in the world happened to all that trouble you thought you were in! It's amazing how trouble shrinks in the presence of God and in the presence of His Word. When you get to the place where you're living your life in the overflow of God's Word, trouble has no space to occupy.

Living in the overflow — that's what will enable us to keep our victory. And that's what we're going to learn how to do in this section of this book. As we said at the beginning, overcoming trouble is not an instantaneaous process. Trouble won't necessarily disappear the minute you start getting yourself filled up with God's Word, or even the minute you start living in the overflow. There's always a period of time between "Amen, I believe I receive..." and "Thank You, Lord, there it is!" There's a space between the faith that says, "I'm healed" or "I'm delivered," and the physical manifestation of whatever you're believing God for.

That space between faith and the answer is usually occupied with trouble and tribulation, tests and trials. Like a defensive line in a football game, trouble often seems to be blocking our way to the answer. Trouble's job is to keep us from scoring. Faith's job is to keep us in the game, to keep us pressing toward the end zone where the promises of God are waiting for us. But it's our job to get in the Word and find out what we must do to get past that tribulation to get to the answer.

There are things we can do on this side of the answer to overcome trouble every time it shows up. There are things we must do to live in the overflow so we can continually walk in the confidence of God even in troubled times.

8

GOD IS IN CONTROL

We live in troubled times. I doubt if anyone would argue with me about that. A glance at a newspaper or a television newscast should convince anyone that if any day qualifies as the time Jesus predicted in Matthew 24, our day does. The events Jesus said would be signs of His coming and of the end of the world seem to be going on all around us.

> **And Jesus answered and said unto them, Take heed that no man deceive you. For many shall come in my name, saying, I am Christ; and shall deceive many. And you shall hear of wars and rumours of wars: see that ye be not troubled: for all these things must come to pass, but the end is not yet. For nation shall rise against nation, and kingdom against kingdom: and there shall be famines, and pestilences, and earthquakes, in divers places. All these are the beginning of sorrows. Then shall they deliver you up to be afflicted, and shall kill you: and ye shall be hated of all nations for my name's sake. And then shall many be offended, and shall betray one another, and shall hate one another. And many false prophets shall rise, and shall deceive many. And because iniquity shall abound, the love of many shall wax cold. But he that shall endure unto the end, the same shall be saved. And this Gospel of the kingdom shall be preached in all the world for a witness unto all nations; and then shall the end come.**
>
> **MATTHEW 24:4-14**

Wars, rumors of wars, famines, pestilences, earthquakes, persecutions, afflictions...we've seen all these terrible manifestations of tribulation in our own day. But did you pick up on what Jesus said right in the middle of this catalog of troubles? If you've been paying attention to what I've been teaching you in this book, you should have. It's right there in verse 6: *See that ye be not troubled!* Here again, Jesus is saying to His disciples, "In the midst of all this trouble, you can have peace. Trouble will come, but you don't have to let it trouble you."

Remember One Thing

Now I know you may still be shaking your head the way you probably were at the beginning of this book and asking, "But, Brother Dollar, how can I help being troubled with all this going on around me? All this fear and anxiety and worry are kind of contagious, you know. I know I shouldn't be anxious, but sometimes it seems like I just can't help it! What can I do not to lose my peace in the middle of all this 'hell on earth'?"

You can keep your peace and walk in fearless confidence even in the midst of these troubled times if you remember one thing: *God is in control.*

God is in control. Child of God, I'm telling you, God's in control of your finances. God's in control of your family and your marriage. God's in control over your job. God is even in control over the devil that's troubling you.

God is in control. Make no mistake about it. The earth is still the Lord's and the fullness thereof (Psalm 24:1). The silver and gold belong to the Lord (Haggai 2:8). The devil's just the god — small *g,* I remind you — over the world system; but God is still God over heaven and earth. And in the name of Jesus, He is about to show you and the rest of this world that He is *still* in control.

God is still in control, and He's the One Who will decide when the end of the world will come. Sure, there's trouble and tribulation in the world, but there always has been. Jesus said **this Gospel of the kingdom shall be preached** in spite of whatever trouble is going on in the end times.

Do you think the Gospel of Jesus Christ, the good news, will roll over and quit just because trouble shows up? No. The Gospel of this kingdom shall be preached. I don't care what trouble arises in this last day. I don't care what's going on in the economic system. I don't care what they're doing in the capitals of all the nations of the world. I don't care what they're doing in the United Nations. *It will not stop the Gospel of Jesus Christ from being preached!*

I don't care what's going on anywhere on the earth — no trouble will stop the Word of God from being preached. This Gospel, this good news, shall be preached in all the world. In the midst of trouble, you will hear the good news of the Lord Jesus Christ. You will always have an option either to be troubled or not to be troubled, but this good news will remain, glory to God.

No Excuse to Curl Up and Die

So now just because trouble is in this world, that doesn't mean we have to curl up and die. It's not a reason for us to give up, cave in and quit. Yes, there are some responsibilities that you and I have to take on. And as I've said all along, troubling our trouble is something we have to *do*.

I'm *not* saying you won't have any more trouble after you begin putting into practice what I'm teaching you in this book. The devil is after your peace, and he will throw up a big mountain of trouble in your path every chance he can get to prevent the Word of God from bearing fruit in your life. There's sometimes a long stretch of country between "Amen, I believe I receive" and the manifestation of the deliverance, healing, safety, protection, provision or whatever it is you're believing God for. But remember, the ultimate victory has already been won. Jesus has overcome the world (John 16:33). God *is* in control, and if we'll do what the Bible tells us to do in between the prayer of faith and the answer, trouble will not be able to overcome us.

Don't Cave In!

One of the biggest enemies of the faith walk is weariness. Often, the answer to our prayers seems to be such a long time coming and there is so much opposition to our attempt to believe God that we become tired of waiting and tired of maintaining our position on the Word. And when we get weary, we can be tempted to give up and quit. The book of Hebrews warns us of the dangers of weariness:

> **For consider him that endured such contradiction of sinners against himself, lest you be wearied and faint in your minds.**

> **HEBREWS 12:3**

According to this Scripture, if you allow yourself to get weary, you will faint in your mind — that is, you will lose the faith fight in your mind.

Why?

Because the mind is the arena of faith. You will lose the battle or you will win it in the arena of your mind.

Now the word *faint*[1] means to what? It means "to give up, cave it, and quit." Therefore, the Bible tells us to consider Jesus — to keep the eye of our faith fixed on Jesus and His Word — because if we don't, we will become weary, and then we will be tempted to faint, to give up, cave in and quit right in the middle of the fight of faith.

Forty Days and Nights on Two Meals

Do you remember the story of how the prophet Elijah called fire down from heaven and triumphed over the prophets of Baal in 1 Kings 18? When Elijah came up against all of those prophets of Baal, the anointing of God was on him. Under that anointing, he called down fire and rain. Under that anointing, he outran Ahab's chariot horses to the gate of the city (1 Kings 18:46).

But the minute Ahab's queen, Jezebel, sent him a message threatening to kill him in revenge for killing her prophets, Elijah got up and ran for his life. He was so scared that he ran a day's journey out into the wilderness and sat down under a juniper tree and prayed that he might die (1 Kings 19:1-4). Two days after he had done mighty miracles, he was so depressed and weary, he was ready to give up and die. What happened?

Elijah forgot to refill. He forgot to fill himself up again with the Word until it overflowed. He allowed himself to become weary, and his weariness gave space for Satan to occupy. Elijah took his eyes off the Word; he didn't replace what he had poured out in doing the miracles, and consequently, the devil was able to come in and put fear in his heart.

God had to send an angel two days in a row to cook Elijah a meal, and he had to eat and drink of this heavenly food before he had the strength to go on again. But when he took the nourishment the Lord sent him, he was able to travel forty days and forty nights on the strength of just those two meals (1 Kings 19:8).

So we must take a lesson from this experience of Elijah's, and remember to keep ourselves nourished with the Word. Otherwise we too may become wearied and faint — give up, cave in and quit — in our minds while we're waiting for the answer to our prayers. No matter how much trouble the devil throws in your way, keep your eyes on Jesus and His Word.

The Key to Getting to the Other Side

There's another reason to keep our eyes on God and His Word in the midst of trouble — it helps us remember that God Himself never gets weary. He never faints and gives up. He is in control over the entire universe. And He has promised that no matter how long we have to wait for the manifestation of what we're believing Him for, as long as we're serving Him while we're waiting, our waiting will never be in vain.

> **Hast thou not known? hast thou not heard, that the everlasting God, the Lord, the Creator of the ends of the earth, fainteth not, neither is weary? there is no searching of his understanding.**
>
> **ISAIAH 40:28**

Isn't it good to know that we have a God in heaven Who will not give up, will not quit and will not cave in? What a perfect Person to make a covenant with, especially when you and I are capable of quitting, giving up and caving in. It would seem only right to cut covenant with Somebody Who won't cave in, give up and quit. In heaven we have a God Who never faints and never gets weary. You can't weary God. Glory to God.

Sometimes we're tempted to think God must be awfully tired of us and our troubles. We think, "God must be getting tired of listening to me. He probably doesn't want to have anything else to do with me. God's fed up with me." Child of God, do you really think your little trouble in your hard time can weary God? How could it? His mercy endures forever. That word *endure* means "to outlast," so that means that His mercy will outlast any trouble.

Anything that you throw at God He can outlast just for the joy of seeing you come into His arms one day and give your life to Him saying, "Lord, I'm yours. Everything I have, everything I've got, everything I am, and everything I'm not, I'm yours."

Renewed Strength

Not only does God never get weary and faint, but He also renews the strength of those who are weary and are at the point of fainting.

> **He giveth power to the faint; and to them that have no might he increaseth strength. Even the youths shall faint and be weary, and the young men shall utterly fall: But they that wait upon the Lord shall renew their strength; they shall mount up with wings as eagles; they shall run, and not be weary; they shall walk and not faint.**

> **ISAIAH 40:29-31**

As you are waiting on the Lord, your strength is renewed. But notice that it's not just your natural strength that's being renewed — your strength is being renewed to the point you can **mount up with wings as eagles.** You won't understand the significance of that until you understand eagles' wings.

A Special Design

An eagle is a bird whose wings are specially designed to enable it to cruise at high altitudes. An eagle can cruise at eighty thousand feet. That's twice as high as jet aircraft normally fly.

The wings of an eagle have been designed to lock down in position to gain altitude so that if the eagle is caught in a storm, it can rise above it. No amount of turbulence can overcome the lock-down position of an eagle's wings because of its ability to rise high. That eagle with locked-down wings will rise higher and higher until it's eventually out of the storm and flying above it. Instead of being in the middle of a storm, the eagle's wings have lifted it up above the storm, and it's out of the turbulent trouble, glory to God.

And so the eagle is no longer a part of the storm, but now he has risen up above that storm. And instead of being subject to the storm, he is now on top of the storm, looking down at it.

Likewise should you and I put on eagles' wings and in the middle of our storms we should rise up to higher altitudes, rise up to greater heights, get above our storm, get above our situation.

In the time of trouble, that's when I will put on my eagle's wings. In the middle of the storm, that's when I will lock them down. And when it gets a little rough, that's when I'll rise above my trouble, above my storms. I don't have to be subject to the storm. I can be riding on high. I can be cruising at a high altitude.

Mount Up!

So mount up. You know, I hear the Word of the Lord say it's time for us to mount up. It's time for us to put on our eagles' wings. It's time for us to get out of this natural world and begin to fly above our situations and circumstances.

You don't have to stay in the middle of your trouble. You don't have to be troubled by your trouble. Yes, you will experience some turbulence, but that's all right. Because the wings are locked down, the turbulence can't hold you back.

You can fly through any storm. There is not a storm that you're not able to come above. I don't care how high the storm is. I don't care how thick the clouds are, God has anointed you with eagles' wings so that you can come up and out and above your circumstances and situations.

Why? *Because God is in control.* We shall mount up with wings as eagles. We shall run and not be weary; we shall walk, and not faint. All because of what I did in the middle of that trouble. All because I got my mind set, kept it set, put guards over my ears and guards over my eyes, and when everybody was calling me too "deep" and "super-spiritual," I was keeping the enemies out of my garden. Yes, I keep the enemies out of my garden. And if trouble shows up, that's all right. I have the ability to rise above the storm. The difference between flying a Lear jet and a twin-engine airplane is whether or not you want to have the ability to rise out of a storm at forty-three thousand feet or ride through it. I have done both. It's a scary thing to ride through a storm. It's a weird kind of thing. But in a jet, you just say, "Hold on a little while. We're coming up and out." And while the people who are still in the storm are reporting over the radio, "There's hail falling; there's wind; there's lightning; there's strong turbulence down here," you're riding on top saying, "There's nothing but sunshine up here."

Set Your Headings

It's time we learned that God has provided the means for us to get out of the storm. It's time for us to lock down our eagles' wings and rise above it. It's time to mount up. Mount up on wings as eagles, and you won't get weary and faint. Set your mind on God's Word.

And don't allow afflictions and persecutions, the cares of this world, the deceitfulness of riches or desires for anything the world system has to offer to distract you from living in the overflow.

Child of God, hear me loud and clear — *God is in control.* Even when you don't think so, God is in control. Even when it looks like everything is going to pieces around you, God is in control.

Remember the widow in the 17th chapter of 1 Kings? That woman was getting ready to die. She said, "I'm going to use up the last of my meal and oil to make this cake for me and my boy. Then we're going to die."

But did her trouble and her fear stop God? Of course not. God stretched the woman's resources. Nobody was putting meal into that barrel. God was stretching the woman's resources. And not only that, later on, this same woman's son got sick and died, but God saw to it that he was revived and resurrected from the dead.

How many of you know God can stretch your resources? Why? Because He's in control. You'd be amazed what two dollars and fifty cents and some coupons can do. God knows how to stretch your resources.

God is in control. "But...but, Pastor, it doesn't look like it."

God is in control.

"But what about my situation?"

God is in control.

"But you don't know what happened last week."

God is in control.

"But the doctor said..."

God is in control.

"But they cut off my..."

God is in control.

"But I don't have..."

God is in control.

"But the devil..."

Shhh. God is in control.

"But they said..."

God is in control!!!

You see, *you* have to know that. *You* must receive that. *You* must believe that in order to maintain your peace. When you can't figure out why things are doing what they're doing, you've got to have in your spirit — "That's all right. God is in control."

I don't understand how this is going to end, but God is in control. I'm not going to fear what might happen because God is in control. I'm not going to fear what man can do to me because God is in control. I'm not going to receive the bad report because God is in control. And if God is in control, it'll be all right.

It'll be all right because it's not you who is in control. You've turned the controls over to God. God's doing the driving. He is responsible for your getting to your proper destination. You'll get there. You'll get there. You'll get there — just keep yourself set. Keep yourself set the way you would set your headings if you were piloting an airplane.

On an airplane you must set your headings because that's the only thing that guarantees you will arrive in the right place. You can't figure it out because when you get up in the air, everything looks the same. But as long as you have your headings set right on your instruments, you don't have to worry about getting lost.

You do the same with the Word of God. Set your headings to take you where you want to go. Then turn control over to the autopilot and sit back and monitor the instruments. Make sure that everything's operating right. God (the Autopilot) will get you to the proper destination. And when you see it, go ahead and land the aircraft. Land it smoothly. Get out and possess the land. Set your headings by the Word of God. Let God do the driving. He's your Autopilot. And then when you get there, just go ahead and possess the land. It's yours. God bought you that. God is in control. Listen to me, child of God — you're going to be all right. From this point on, you don't have to be troubled. Trouble may show up, but you don't have to let it trouble you. The devil may claim to be in control of your circumstances, but you can just laugh in his face and say, "Get out of here, devil. You're not in control. God is in control. Nobody but Jesus sits on the throne of my life. And because

Jesus sits there, I will have righteousness. I will have peace. I will have joy in the Holy Ghost. I bind principalities and powers and wicked spirits in heavenly places, and God is perfecting that which concerns me. In Jesus' name. Amen."

---

[1] James Strong, "Greek Dictionary of the New Testament," *Strong's Exhaustive Concordance of the Bible,* (Nashville: Abingdon, 1890), p. 26, #1590.

9

DOING OUR PART

In the previous chapter, we said one of the reasons we can walk in the confidence of God during troubled times is that God is in control. But God's being in control doesn't mean that we have no part in the process of troubling our trouble. Overcoming trouble is not just God's responsibility. We also have a responsibility and a part to play. There are things we have to do in order for the system God has put in place to operate in our lives.

Therefore, in this chapter, we are going to zero in on our responsibility during trouble, on *our* responsibility for doing the things of God. As you read the Scriptures I'm going to share with you, I want you to ask yourself, "What is my responsibility, my part in this process? What do I have to do to apply God's Word to my life so that I can walk in the confidence of God in troubled times?"

First, let's review some things we've already covered. Remember, in John 16:33, Jesus said:

> These things I have spoken unto you, that in me ye might have peace. In the world ye shall have tribulation: but be of good cheer; I have overcome the world.

Again, we don't make light of the trouble that has already invaded this planet. Without a doubt you see troubles everywhere. All kinds of things are happening like the things Jesus described in the 24th chapter of Matthew. But in John 16:33, Jesus says something very significant. He says, "I've spoken to you that in Me you might have peace." That reminds me that the Book of Isaiah says that God has established a covenant of peace (Isaiah 54:10).

God's Part, Satan's Part and Our Part

God has done His part by establishing this covenant of peace. Now Satan's job, his part, is to attempt to keep us from inheriting this covenant, to keep us from operating in it or walking in it. So God has done His part, and Satan wants to do his part, but we must learn to do our part. Yes, we do have a part.

I heard a story one time about a man who saw the devil sitting on a wall outside a church, crying. The man said, "What's the matter, Satan? Why are you crying?" And the devil said, "I'm tired of these Christians lying about me. I'm tired of them blaming me for all their trouble. I'm getting blamed for stuff I didn't even do!"

The point is, you must understand that it is your job to take responsibility for what is and is not happening in your life. You have responsibility.

Whatsoever a man soweth, that shall he also reap.

GALATIANS 6:7

What is Paul saying? He's saying, *a man's condition in life is based purely on the seeds that he has sown in the past.* So if you don't like your condition, change it. How? By changing the seeds that you sow.

The Word Brings Peace

Jesus said:

These things I have spoken...that *in me* ye might have peace.

JOHN 16:33

Now, would it be correct for me to say, "In the Word you might have peace"? I can say that because John 1:1 says:

In the beginning was the Word, and the Word was with God, and the Word was God.

I can say, "that in the Word you might have peace" because the Word gave birth to Jesus, and the Word has also given birth to peace.

God is interested in our inheriting this covenant of peace. But we have to be watchful because there are certain wiles, certain tricks, the devil will try to use on us. And most of us have fallen into the devil's traps. But we're going to learn how to get out of the trap.

Seek the Things Above

Colossians 3:1 says:

If ye then be risen with Christ [the Anointed One and His Anointing]**, seek those things which are above, where Christ** [the Anointed One and His Anointing] **sitteth on the right hand of God.**

Now is Paul talking about seeking something that's over your head? No, he's talking about seeking something that's higher. *The Amplified Bible* says to seek **the higher things** (v. 2), that is, seek something that's on a higher level.

And so we understand that the Word of God is higher than the world system. Things that are above are found in the Word of God. You won't be able to get hold of those things that are above if you don't get in the Word. You can't read your Bible just on Sunday.

You can't be a Christian just on Sunday because the devil has Monday through Saturday to get you unless you make a decision to get into the Word of God every day.

Paul goes on:

> **Set your affection on things above, not on things on the earth. For ye are dead, and your life is hid with Christ in God.**

COLOSSIANS 3:2,3

The Amplified Bible says:

> **If then you have been raised with Christ [to a new life, thus sharing His resurrection from the dead], aim at and seek the [rich, eternal treasures] that are above, where Christ is, seated at the right hand of God.**

> **And set your minds and keep them set on what is above (the higher things), not on the things that are on the earth.**

> **For [as far as this world is concerned] you have died, and your [new, real] life is hidden with Christ in God.**

COLOSSIANS 3:1-3, AMP

Set your mind and keep it set. Now whose responsibility is that? God's or yours? Can you pray "Heavenly Father, I pray in the name of Jesus that You set my mind and keep it set on Your Word"? Will God do that for you? No, He won't.

What about this prayer? "Lord, humble me." Do you think He's going to humble you? No. "Lord, please, in the name of Jesus, make me read my Word." Is He going to do that? *No!*

You see, we've been walking around in this false humility thinking God will do all this stuff, and I'm telling you that it is your responsibility. And until you take some responsibility for your life as a Christian, there are certain things God will not do because He has placed the responsibility in your hands and in my hands. God won't pick up the Book and read it to you while you sleep.

You have to read the Bible for yourself. There are certain things that have happened in our lives that are not God's fault. They're not the devil's fault. They're your fault; they're my fault. It is our fault these things have happened because we failed to take responsibility for our actions. And we have failed to do our part so God could do His part to make the system operate as it needs to operate.

Not on Earthly Things

Colossians 3:2 warns us not to set our minds on the things of the earth. And there is a reason why God doesn't want us to set our minds on things on earth. He doesn't want us watching television news twenty-four hours a day because if we do, what will our minds be set on? All the cares of this world.

Child of God, Satan wants to infiltrate you with the cares of this world. He wants you to hear the words that promote the cares of this world. He wants you to hear his words because the words of the devil will produce fear. However, the Word of God will produce faith.

John 14:27 says:

Peace I leave with you, my peace I give unto you: not as the world giveth, give I unto you. Let not your heart be troubled, neither let it be afraid.

Let me point out three things here. First, you are responsible for your heart. You have responsibility for what goes into you. The devil may be trying to put something in you, but you're still responsible for what gets into your heart through your ears and through your eyes. Secondly, Jesus says here that you have the responsibility for making sure your heart is not troubled. And thirdly, He says you have the responsibility for making sure your heart is not filled with fear. You are responsible for seeing to it that your heart is not troubled or afraid.

It's important not to let your heart be filled with fear because where there is no fear, there can be no trouble. Trouble may be around, but if you aren't filled with fear, you won't be troubled by it. Even though trouble may be present, your heart won't be troubled if it isn't afraid.

The Sources of Fear and Faith

Where does fear come from? Well, where does faith come from?

Faith cometh by hearing, and hearing by the word of God.

ROMANS 10:17

The reciprocal of that statement is that fear comes by hearing the words of the devil. The devil wants you to hear his words. Because he is god of the world system, he wants you to hear the words that come from the world system. He wants you to fill your heart with his words so you will operate in fear which is inverted faith.

Pay close attention to what I'm saying. *To walk in fear is to walk in faith.* If you fear cancer, what you're actually doing is having faith and confidence in the ability of cancer to kill you. If you fear losing your job because of a wrong report about you, you're actually having faith and confidence in the ability of that wrong report to cause you to lose your job. If you fear being mugged when you go to the ATM machine at night, you have faith and confidence in the ability of that mugger to attack and rob you.

When you operate in fear, you're operating in the faith and confidence that the thing you fear has the ability to destroy you.

The Faith of the Devil

So you have to reverse the process. Instead of having fear that the devil can do a certain thing in your life, you must have faith in the Word of God. Your faith is a force which will produce whatever is in your heart. Whatever is in your heart will motivate you to give room for either God or the devil to bring that thing to pass. I know it sounds strange, *but fear is the faith of the devil.* Fear is what the devil needs in order to bring certain things to pass in your life.

Where is the fear in your life? Wherever the fear is in your life, you must move it because if you don't move it, you have left a door open for the devil to say, "I have the right to bring the thing that they fear to pass." And whatever is in your heart that's producing fear probably outweighs the Word of God. That means it takes precedence over the Word of God because you're more filled with the stuff you fear than you are with the Word of God.

The Importance of Guarding Our Hearts

So what is the devil trying to do here? Why is it so important that I guard my heart? It's important because it's the difference between being troubled and being trouble-free. Can you recall certain times when you wish you hadn't heard certain things? Your day was going fine; you were having a wonderful time, then somebody told you something you wish they had just kept to themselves until the end of the day. And what happened? That bad report, those unpleasant things, invaded your heart and occupied your thinking even though you might have just gotten out of Bible study. What was the devil doing to you?

To find out, let's look again at what Jesus said in Mark 4.

> **The sower soweth the word. And these are they by the way side, where the word is sown; but when they have heard, Satan cometh immediately, and taketh away the word that was sown in their hearts. And these are they likewise which are sown on stony ground; who, when they have heard the word, immediately receive it with gladness; And have no root in themselves, and so endure but for a time: afterward, when affliction or persecution ariseth for the word's sake, immediately they are offended. And these are they which are sown among thorns; such as hear the word, And the cares of this world, and the deceitfulness of riches, and the lusts of other things entering in, choke the word, and it becometh unfruitful.**

> **MARK 4:14-19**

There it is, right there in verse 19:

> **The cares of this world...choke the word, and it becometh unfruitful.**

The cares of this world have the ability to choke the Word, to make it unfruitful.

Listen to me, child of God, Satan wants to fill your heart with the cares of this world. He wants to use the cares in your life, your marriage, your family, your job, the news to get you full of care. Then even though you're going to church and reading the Bible, those cares choke up what little bit of Word you get.

That's why you need to get more Word than what you get just on Sundays. Some of you are being defeated, not because you're not getting the Word, but because you're getting more care than you are Word. Therefore, you never see your harvest because the cares of this world are in you so abundantly that they choke up what Word you get. There isn't enough Word to overcome the cares you're receiving.

You have all day long six days a week to receive cares. But you take only one day out of the week for a couple of hours to receive Word. So the cares are choking the Word.

Until the Word becomes a life, it will never become a reality. The cares of this world enter in and choke the Word so it cannot bring forth the fruit it was designed to bring forth. You're so busy dealing with the cares of the world, (your world), that you don't take in enough Word. And the cares you're filled with occupy your attention and distract you from the Word.

Negative Meditation

Most of us have spent all our lives carrying around the cares of the world as if we could actually do something about them! We've been carrying cares around as if we knew how to handle them, when actually all we do when we carry care around is get ourselves in a position where the Word of God becomes unfruitful.

The cares of the world choke the Word until you spend all your time feeding off the cares of the world. You spend all your time meditating on fear and on what *could* happen in this or that situation. It hasn't even happened yet, but you're worrying about it; you're meditating on *what* might happen. That's what worry is. Worry is a negative form of meditation.

What does Joshua 1:8 say about meditation? It says if you meditate on the Word day and night, you'll make your way prosperous and have success. Well, guess what happens when you worry on the word of the devil day and night!

When you worry on the word of the devil day and night, you will make yourself prosperous and successful in the things of the devil.

For instance, if you worry that your son will become a drug addict, you'll prosper in that; you'll have good success in that, and pretty soon you'll have a cocaine addict in your household.

Why? You meditated on it. Your son became a drug addict because you engaged in negative meditation, and that fear — the faith of the devil — directed the forces in your heart in the wrong way, and those forces produced results in your life.

Don't Wait

"Well, Brother Dollar, I thought it was just natural to worry. How can you do anything to keep from worrying? I don't think it's possible not to worry." Yes, at the moment it may seem impossible to do anything else except worry, but why is that? It's because you are trying to wait until the last minute before you cram the Word in.

Don't wait until the doctor tells you that you're about to die before you cram the Word in. Don't wait until you're bombarded with trouble before you begin cramming the Word in. Filling your heart with the Word must be a lifestyle so you can live it day by day by day. But most of us walk around with our hearts more filled with the cares of the world than with the Word of God. The little time we spend in God's Word is causing us to miss out on some valuable things because we don't think we *really* have to do all that it takes to fill our hearts to the point of overflow. We make up our famous excuses, "Well, you know, God understands."

What God Understands

Oh yes, He understands that you're not going to get what you're believing Him for *because you have not done your part to make it happen.* "Well, you know, God understands the reason why I didn't tithe." Yes, He understands that the heavens are closed to you, and the devourer will not be rebuked for your sake. And He understands that it's no wonder your car stays torn up all the time because you don't give Him the tithe that will give Him permission and position in your life to rebuke the devil and say, "Stop. No more. You can't touch their pipes. You can't touch their car. When the winter storm comes, the tree can't fall on their house."

Now, I'm not saying a tree fell on your house because you were out of position with God. But if you're tithing and doing what you're supposed to do, then regardless of what happens, God has already made a way out. He's already fixed things so they'll work the way they're supposed to work. God has done His part. But you have to do your part. You have to spend more time in the Word than you do in meditating on the cares of the world most of which you can't do anything about anyway!

I'm Not Paid to Know That!

Somebody came up to me one time and said, "Did you know Michael Jackson got married?" I looked at him kind of as if to say, "Is he giving me money to know? Is he going to write me a check to know?" No, I didn't know. I didn't care. I spend my time in the Word of God, getting fed the Word of God and getting built up in the Holy Ghost. I don't care whether some entertainer got married. That's none of my business. Now if I were being paid to know, I'd know. But otherwise, my knowing he got married isn't going to help me. My question is, "Did you know that by His stripes we are healed?"

Did You Know...?

Do you know that God says He knows how to deliver us out of all our trouble? Did you know that we have a secret place of the Most High? Did you know that there's power in the name of Jesus? Did you know that the anointing will give me victory? How about getting in the good news of the Gospel and laying some of this gossip to rest!

I don't care if you spend your time watching television soap operas. But if you do, when you get in trouble, you'll have to come to me to get help because while you were spending time filling your heart with the cares of the world, I was spending time filling my heart with the Word of God. I was confessing that Word every day, writing it on my heart every day, listening to teaching and preaching tapes in my car every day.

But you're in trouble because you think, "It doesn't take all that. God understands I have a career, and I don't have time for the Word." No. God does not understand that. He understands that you have made your career a god instead of Him. *That's* what He understands. He understands you're filling yourself with the cares of this world instead of with the Word of God.

The Only Place for Care

According to the Bible, there is only one thing we are anointed to do with care, and that is to cast it on God.

Humble yourselves therefore under the mighty hand of God, that he may exalt you in due time:

Casting all your care upon him; for he careth for you.

1 PETER 5:6,7

Humble yourselves.... We first must exercise biblical humility. As simply as I can put it, Bible humility is to do what God said to do. Humility is submission, compliance, submission of yourself to the commandments of God. To disobey God's commands is spiritual rebellion and pride. Biblical humility, on the other hand, is to submit oneself to comply with and carry out the commandments of God Almighty.

We are to humble ourselves **under the mighty hand of God.** Now as we saw in chapter 8, when Elijah got under the hand of God, he outran horses and chariots to the entrance of Jezreel (1 Kings 18:46). So Peter is saying that when you get under the mighty hand of God, you can expect some anointing. You can expect some power. And when you submit yourself to God, you are submitting yourself to His Word. You are to consider the Word before you consider the cares of this world because the Word has anointing to it. The Word has power to it.

God wants to exalt you. He wants you submitted under His hand so that **He may exalt you in due time.** There's one thing we know about "due season" *It always comes.* But when will you be exalted? When you get yourself in a position to be exalted. And that position is in humility under the commandments of God.

If you step out from under the hand of God and say, "I'm going to do what I want to do," you will get yourself in a position to fall. But when you let God bring you up, He becomes the One responsible for the support to maintain you in that higher position.

Humble yourselves...that he may exalt you...

1 PETER 5:6

And here comes the point I wanted us to get to:

Casting all your care upon him; for he careth for you.

1 PETER 5:7

How many cares? *All your care.* Cast your family care, your job care, your financial care, your physical care, your spiritual care, cast it all on God. The Bible says cast all your care on Him.

Well, why don't you do it?

Get Rid of It!

Who do you think you are, walking around maintaining the cares of your life as if you are anointed to do something about them? You have never been anointed to do something about your cares except one thing: To cast them! Cast them on the Lord! That's the only thing He's anointed you to do with your cares. Cast them. *Casting* in fishing means that when you cast that rod out, the line out, it goes from you to another place.

"Do you mean, Preacher, that I'm supposed to get rid of this care?" Yes, I mean that.

And do you know why?

Because God wants to get rid of it, and He can't get rid of it until you get rid of it. You're not supposed to be walking around full of care. God is saying to you, "Cast your cares on Me. I'm equipped to handle your cares. I am anointed to handle your care. I know what to do with your cares. I know how to destroy your cares. If you'll just let Me, I will demonstrate that I know what I'm doing."

It's an act of rebellion for you to maintain your cares, trying to figure out what to do and how to fix a problem yourself. "Oh, dear Lord, how am I going to do this?" Hold it — you're not supposed to know how to do it. You're supposed to get rid of it. That care is not your problem. It is not your responsibility. And you grieve the Spirit of God because you stop Him from doing what He desires to do with your cares. Don't walk around in your false humility, saying, "Well, I'll be all right after a while." No, no. You could be all right now by faith if you would cast those cares away.

Not on the Pastor!

The Bible says to cast your cares on the Lord. It doesn't say cast them on the pastor of your church. Some times Christians think they should dump everything on the pastor or the deacons or the counselors. And as a pastor, I've had to learn to get up in the morning and say, "Good morning, Jesus. I don't care." Then when people in my congregation try to dump their problems on me, I can avoid taking someone else's cares, cares which don't belong to me. I'm not supposed to carry my own cares, much less anyone else's. The Bible doesn't say bring all your cares to the pastor. It says to cast your cares on God because He cares for you.

God cares for you much more than I could ever think about caring for you. Hallelujah! Don't give your cares to me because I don't know what to do with them. They might come back on you if you give them to me.

I can't take on other people's problems. That's not my job. The Bible tells me not to do that.

Someone called my office one day and said, "You tell Pastor Dollar that he's a racist."

And I thought, "Oh, God, here we go again. Why do you say I'm a racist?"

"Because you said *honkey* on TV."

"Well, as I remember, I also said *nigger*."

"But you're a racist. You don't like white folks."

Well, if I don't like white folks, I'm in a lot of trouble because I adopted one! But this caller didn't know that.

Imagine what would happen to my peace if I take that care and worry about people calling me a racist, and all week long everytime I pass somebody white, I say, "I'm not a racist. I'm not a racist. I'm really not a racist." I might just as well get a sign to carry around which says, "I'm not a racist."

Do you see why I can't do that? I don't have the ability to get before people and defend myself against a rumor. That's not my job. My job is just to be in Christ, and cast my care on Him and let Him take care of it.

10

THE KEY TO SUCCESS

All the way through this book I've been trying to convince you that even though trouble may be all around you, you don't have to be troubled by the trouble. However, let me repeat that it's not my intention to imply that trouble will disappear off the face of the earth just because you learn to use the weapons we have available to trouble our trouble. My objective is to teach you to use those weapons so that you can overcome trouble. Trouble will be here, but you don't have to be troubled by your trouble.

Also, we have talked about our own responsibility in troubling our trouble. There are certain things we have to do ourselves to make sure we are not overcome by trouble: Quit blaming the devil, quit blaming other people and accept responsibility for what's happening and what's going on. We must do these things because in the beginning, God gave man first dominion and authority, and then second, He gave man seed. Now why did He do that? He gave us these gifts so that we can be responsible for our own outcomes, our own position in life and for things that concern us. But that means we must take some responsibility since we have been given the authority to do so.

Therefore, if we are to be successful in troubling our trouble and walking in the confidence of God during troubled times, we must do our part. But our level of success will be determined by our confidence level in God and in His Word. The degree of confidence you have in God's Word will determine the degree of your success in this life in the middle of trouble.

No Word, No Confidence

Having absolute confidence in God and His Word is the key to success in overcoming trouble in every area of your life. The Book of Hebrews makes that clear.

> **Cast not away therefore your confidence, which hath great recompence of reward.**

> **HEBREWS 10:35**

Don't cast your confidence away! Don't get rid of it. Well, how does a man cast away his confidence? When he casts away the Word of God. If you don't have the Word of God on a certain subject, you won't have confidence in that particular subject.

For instance, if you don't have the Word of God on the subject of sowing and reaping, you won't have confidence in sowing because you won't have confidence in reaping. If you don't have the Word of God on divine health and divine healing, you won't experience it.

Why?

Because there is no confidence.

That's why **faith cometh by hearing, and hearing by the Word of God** (Romans 10:17). That's why it's of such great importance to hear the Word of God so you can get confidence in those things that the Bible talks about. If you don't have any Word, you definitely won't have confidence.

The Amplified Bible puts it like this:

> **Do not, therefore, fling away your fearless confidence, for it carries a great and glorious compensation of reward.**

> **HEBREWS 10:35, AMP**

The Bible is saying that a man who holds fast to his confidence, a man who holds fast to the Word of God, can expect to be compensated for holding on to his confidence. He will be compensated for holding to the Word. When you hold on to your confidence, when you hold on to the Word, then you're holding a guarantee of compensation. It pays to keep the Word in your life. You lose when you don't.

The Reward of Diligence in the Word

Let me show you a man who held on to his confidence in the Word and was compensated for his diligence in the Word. This man is described in Psalm 112:

Praise ye the Lord. Blessed is the man that feareth the Lord, that delighteth greatly in his commandments.

v. 1

Now we need to give a little attention to the word *bless* before we go on. That word *bless*[1] means "empowered to prosper." And the word *prosper* means being in control of your circumstances and situations, or being in control to excel to a certain point. It's the empowerment I want to zero in on here.

The fact that I am empowered simply means that I have been given ability. I've been empowered. Power has been given. Ability has been given. I've been empowered to be in control of my outcome through the dominion and the seed that God has given.

Psalm 112:1 specifically talks about a man who is empowered through his delight in the Word of God. This man is delighting in the commandments of God, and the Bible says through his delight, he's empowered. But how is it that a man can be empowered by just delighting in the commandments of God? You know, the Bible says "delight yourself in the Lord and He will give you" what? "the desires of your heart" (Psalm 37:4).

Something happens to a man who delights in the Word of God. This man in Psalm 112 is empowered; he is blessed because he delights greatly in the Word of God. And as a result of his delight in God's Word:

> **His seed shall be mighty upon the earth: the generation of the upright shall be blessed.**
>
> v. 2

Now he's blessed; he's been empowered with the Word of God. He's been empowered with those things that come from delighting in God's Word.

> **Wealth and riches shall be in his house: and his righteousness endureth for ever.**
>
> v. 3

Somebody says, "Say what?" Yes, you're reading the right thing. It says, "A man who will delight in the commandments of God sets himself up for wealth and riches to be in his house: and his righteousness endures for ever."

Well, is there a Scripture in the New Testament which verifies that? Yes, Matthew 6:33:

> **Seek ye first the kingdom of God, and his righteousness; and all these things shall be added unto you.**

We've been doing everything except the right things to get the things we need. And the right thing we must do to get the things is to delight ourselves in the Word of God. While you're trying to figure out how to get all of these physical needs met, you could be delighting yourself in the Word of God. Delight yourself in the Word because it is responsible for putting those physical things in your life.

Light in the Darkness

The psalmist continues:

Unto the upright there ariseth light in the darkness.

PSALM 112:4

Now who is that upright man? He's the same man who delights in the commandments of God. The man who delights in God's Word will have light in the darkness. Let me show you what that means.

How many of you have had an idea, and you just thought you were the smartest person in the whole world? You just pat yourself on the back; you're walking around saying, "I'm good! I'm good!"

Let me tell you, "No, you're not!" The only reason you got that great idea is because you've been spending all that time in God's Word. But the man who delights in the commandments of God — the man who studies, meditates and confesses the Word on a daily basis — doesn't fear darkness.

Why?

Because God promises that the man who delights in His Word will always have light arising right in the middle of darkness.

Hanging Around in God's Word

When you hang around in God's Word and delight yourself in the commandments of God, the revelation-understanding light of God will explode on the inside of you. And God says to you, "I'll guarantee you there will *not* be a time where you will *not* know what to do; even if you don't understand it in the natural, I'll give you light in the midst of darkness! Just because you've delighted yourself in My Word." Hallelujah! Glory to God!

I've solved problems which I had no understanding of at all. And have received enlightenment about things I didn't know anything about in the natural. Where did that light come from? It came from the time I had spent in the Word *before* that thing came up.

You see, sometimes you can be riding in the car, trying to figure something out, and the answer will just pop up! Did it just pop up because you're smart? No! *It popped up because you have been spending time in the Word of God, and that Word has gotten on the inside of you, and God has promised that in darkness light shall rise!* So, the idea, the answer to the problem, is compensation for time spent in the Word.

Don't you know God is faithful? He is faithful to pay you what's due to you. Compensation for time spent in the Word. Child of God, you're not spending time in the Word for free! God says, "I'll compensate you if you don't cast away your check!" He says, "I'll cash it if you don't throw it away." Compensation, compensation. It's wonderful to know that in the middle of darkness, for the upright man who has been delighting in God's Word, light will rise. If you have not yet had times where you were in the dark and didn't know what to do, just wait — you'll have those times. And it's good to know that you've done what you needed to do before that time comes to get the compensation of the light.

Free From Fear

A good man sheweth favour, and lendeth: he will guide his affairs with discretion.

Surely he shall not be moved for ever: the righteous shall be in everlasting remembrance.

He shall not be afraid of evil tidings: his heart is fixed, trusting in the Lord.

His heart is established, he shall not be afraid, until he see his desire upon his enemies.

PSALM 112:5-8

The man who delights in the Word of God will not be afraid. How is it that he is not afraid? His heart is fixed. There it is. This man has a fixed heart. What do you think it's fixed on? The Word of God. And because he has a fixed heart, he is also free from fear. I'll tell you why you have fear in your heart. Because you don't have the Word in your heart. That's simple, isn't it? If you don't have the Word in your heart, then the devil will immediately try to occupy that void area. But when your heart is fixed on the Word, you're able to trust in the Lord, and neither will you fear.

That's what the Bible is talking about in John 14:27, when Jesus said, **Let not your heart be troubled, neither let it be afraid.** And we must accept the responsibility given to us through that Scripture. It is our responsibility to not be afraid, and to let not our heart be troubled. Our responsibility is to fix our hearts. Our responsibility is to get our hearts fixed on the Word of God.

Practical Application

Now, I want to show you how to do that, practically. I don't want to just tell you to "Get your heart fixed, because you know...." People don't do cartwheels when you tell them, "Meditate in the Word of God, and that'll solve your problem."

People don't do cartwheels when you tell them, "Spend eight hours a day for five days in the Word of God, and you'll get healed." They don't do that! This generation wants everything right now!

A heart that is fixed, a heart that is established on the Word of God. How do I do it? How do I get my heart fixed and established on the Word of God? I do it by having Scriptures that I say out loud every day. I try to say these Scriptures two to three times a day out loud.

Things I Don't Want to Go Through

And what happens is this: I've recognized that there are just certain things in life I don't want to go through. Somebody says, "But what if you have to go through this, what would you do?" Well, I don't know what I would do, so I don't want to go through it. I don't want anybody coming in telling me I've got some kind of deadly disease, or that I have cancer or I'm going to die in three months. Therefore, I believe in the preventive method. I believe in preventing those things.

"What if you just all went broke?" Well, I don't want to go through that, so I like the preventive way. If I don't know the answers to those things, then I'll be afraid; I'll be troubled; I'll get worried. And then after awhile fear will come in. And I will pretend to be a man of faith, but I'll actually be fearing on the inside.

I learned something in a troubled time in my life, where I felt like I was going to crumble, give up and cave in, and the Lord spoke to my heart, "Practice what you preach." So I did it, and it has been working for me all this time.

The Answer to All Problems

Maybe I'm taking it a little bit far, but I absolutely believe with all my heart that the answer to any or all of my problems is to make sure my heart is fixed on the Word on a daily basis. The Bible says in Colossians, **Set your minds and keep them set** (Colossians 3:2, AMP). I believe it! I set my heart, I keep my mind set, I keep this stuff in my heart. I absolutely believe that I am controlling a successful and victorious destination, because I refuse to let a day go by without fixing my heart. Now, I've got a day of peace. Now, I've got a day worry-free. I have no anxiety. It doesn't matter what happens during that day because I can rely on what I have done in my heart every day.

Now somebody says, "Well, you know, it doesn't take all that." Yes, I believe it does take all of what I'm getting ready to show you! And I don't believe that one hour a week in church on Sunday is enough to cause me to live a successful, victorious Christian life! I believe it takes a commitment, a daily commitment, until my heart is operating in the overflow. Glory to God!

Daily Confessions:[2] Worry and Fear

I have something that I say over worry and fear every day. It sounds like this:

"I am the Body of Christ and Satan has no power over me, for I overcome evil with good. I am of God and have overcome Satan, for greater is He that is in me than he that is in the world. I will fear no evil, for thou art with me. The Lord, Your Word, Your Spirit, they comfort me. I am far from oppression, and fear does not come nigh me. And I won't be depressed today, either, Lord. No weapon formed against me shall prosper, for my righteousness is of the Lord. But whatsoever I do will prosper, for I am like a tree that's planted by the rivers of water. I am delivered from the evils of this present world, for it is the will of God concerning me that I be delivered from the evil of this present world. No evil will befall me, neither shall any plague come near my dwelling, for the Lord has given His angels charge over me, and they keep me in all my ways. And in my pathway is life, and there is no death. I'm not dying any time soon, devil.

"I am a doer of the Word of God, and I'm blessed in my deeds. I am happy in those things which I do, because I'm a doer of the Word of God! I take the shield of faith, which is the Word of God, and I quench every fiery dart that the wicked one brings against me. Christ has redeemed me from the curse of the law; therefore, I forbid any sickness or disease to come upon this body. Every disease and germ and every virus that touches this body dies instantly, in the name of Jesus. Every organ and every tissue of this body functions in the perfection in which God created it to function. I forbid any malfunction in this body, in the name of Jesus! I am an overcomer, and I overcome by the blood of the Lamb and the word of my testimony.

"I am submitted to God, and the devil flees from me, because I resist him in the name of Jesus. The Word of God is forever settled in heaven; therefore, I establish His Word upon this earth. Great is the peace of my children, for they are taught of the Lord."

Weight Control

To control my weight, so I won't overeat, I confess:

"I don't desire to eat so much that I become over-weight. I present my body to God; my body is the temple of the Holy Ghost, which dwelleth in me. I am not my own; I am bought with a price; therefore, in the name of Jesus, I refuse to overeat! Body, settle down, in the name of Jesus, and conform to the Word of God. I mortify, kill, put to death the desires of this body, and command it to come in line with the Word of God!"

Material Needs

Here is a confession for material needs, so you won't ever lack anything:

"Christ has redeemed me from the curse of the law! Christ has redeemed me from poverty! Christ has redeemed me from sickness! Christ has redeemed me from spiritual death. For poverty, He has given me wealth. For sickness, He has given me health. For death, He has given me eternal life! It is true unto me according to the Word of God, and I delight myself in the Lord, and He gives me the desires of my heart. And I have given, and it is given unto me, good measure, pressed down, shaken together, running over, shall men give unto my bosom. For with what mea-sure I mete, it is measured unto me. And I sow bountifully; therefore, I reap bountifully! I give cheerfully, and my God has made all grace abound towards me, and I, having all sufficiency for all things, do abound to all good works!

There is no lack, for my God has supplied all my needs according to His riches in glory! The Lord is my shepherd, and I do not want! Because Jesus was made poor, that I through His poverty, might have abundance. For He came that I might have life and have it more abundantly! And I, having received abundance of grace and the gift of righteousness, do reign as king in life by Jesus Christ! And the Lord has pleasure in the prosperity of His servant, that's me! And Abraham's blessings are mine!"

Wisdom and Guidance

And then I have one for wisdom and guidance:

"The Spirit of truth abideth in me, and teaches me all things, and He guides me into truth. Therefore, I confess I have perfect knowledge, perfect knowledge of every situation, and every circumstance that I come up against, for I have the wisdom of God. I trust in the Lord with all my heart, and I lean not unto my own understanding. In all my ways I acknowledge Him and He directs my path. The Lord will perfect that which concerneth me! I let the Word of Christ dwell in me richly in all wisdom. And I do follow the Good Shepherd, and I know His voice, and the voice of a stranger I will not follow!

"Jesus is made unto me wisdom and righteousness, sanctification, redemption, therefore, I confess I have the wisdom of God, and I am the righteousness of God in Christ Jesus! I am filled with the knowledge of the Lord's will in all wisdom and spiritual understanding! I am a new creation in Christ! I am His workmanship, created in Christ

Jesus, therefore, I have the mind of Christ, and the wisdom of God is formed within me. I have put off the old man and have put on the new man, which was renewed in knowledge after the image of Him that created me! I have received the spirit of wisdom and revelation in the knowledge of Him. The eyes of my understanding are being enlightened! And I am not conformed to this world, but I am transformed by the renewing of my mind! My mind is renewed with the Word of God, and I am increasing in the knowledge of God, and I am strengthened with all might according to His glorious power in Jesus' name!"

The Results

I just go on and on and on for about 20 minutes. And when I get up, I fear nothing! My heart is fixed. My heart is fixed, trusting in the Lord.

Tongue and Heart

Why do I need to say it out loud? There are people who get upset with this confession business. "Why do you have to say it out loud? Why can't you say it to yourself?" Because your mouth is involved with your heart. If you're going to get your heart fixed, you're going to need your mouth to do it.

My tongue is the pen of a ready writer.

PSALM 45:1

My son, forget not my law; but let thine heart keep my commandments....Write them upon the table of thine heart.

PROVERBS 3:1,3

In order to write God's commandements on my heart, I have to use my tongue. If the tongue is the pen and my heart is the table, then I must use my mouth to write the Word on my heart.

So I get my heart fixed on the Word of God concerning my life for that particular day by saying it out loud. I'll spend some time praying. And when I pray, I'll spend some time confessing the Word over every area that I know of in my life, so I can speak the Word of God to that area and fill my heart with that Word.

"Well, I don't think you need to do all that!" That's why you keep having those problems every day, as a result of the fear that you have, as a result of the negative information that came through your ears. So I set myself up differently. When the negative information comes through my ears, the Word of God should rise up and meet it head-on, and say, "You can't affect him. Get out of here! I was here first."

As the result of saying the Word out loud, you have filled your heart with it to the point that Satan's words can find no room to occupy. The overflow of the Word just washes the devil's words right out.

I Dare You!

Confessing the Word out loud is actually putting Jesus on the throne of your life and putting the Word in your heart. *This is something very practical that every believer can do.*

I *dare* you to do this! If you're worrying, put enough Word in you concerning not being anxious, so when the temptation to worry comes up, the Word meets it head-on and says, "Not today! Not today!" When you're fearing that you're not going to be able to pay that bill, but you've already confessed the Word concerning provision and prosperity and have written it on your heart, the Word will meet the fear of lack head-on and say, "No, you'll not affect them today!" When the temptation to overeat and the spirit of gluttony assaults you, the first thing that rises up before you order that next plate will be, "Nope! Can't do it, not there!"

Where Success Begins

I'm telling you, when you put the Word in your heart, it will compensate you for the time spent in the Word of God! The entire situation in your life can change if you'll just do this very practical, simple exercise that I just showed you every day of your life. I dare you to do it! I already know it works.

And don't confine yourself just to the Scriptures on protection, prosperity and healing. Find Scriptures for your own circumstances and your own situation.

For instance, you might be a man who is afraid of being fired or of losing his job, or a man who is afraid of not being able to support his family. In that case, you need to look up all the Scriptures about who *God said you are.* You need to meditate on those Scriptures on the favor of God and how, once God opens the door, no man can close the door that God has opened. Soon you'll have yourself so built up in confidence that even though you were the last one hired, you'll say to the man who was the first one hired,

"I'm going to keep my job. Even if the company closes, they'll offer *me* a job!"

Child of God, that's success. Success begins in a man's heart. Success doesn't begin on the outside; it begins on the inside. If you don't have success in your heart, you won't have success. Success is determined by what's going on inside of you.

Psalm 119 says:

> **Remember the word unto thy servant, upon which thou hast caused me to hope.**
>
> **This is my comfort in my affliction: for thy word hath quickened me.**
>
> **vv. 49, 50**

What is the psalmist's comfort in his affliction? The Word of God.

In the midst of your trouble, in the midst of your affliction, you shall find comfort in the Word of God. In the midst of trouble, you can open the Bible and begin to meditate in the Word. You can begin to confess the Word, and your problems will be reduced to little tiny situations, that you didn't notice were that small until you put them next to the success in God's Word.

---

[1] *The American Heritage Dictionary of the English Language,* (New York: Houghton Mifflin, 1970), p. 141.

[2] I am indebted to Charles Capps for these daily confessions which I learned from his book, *God's Creative Power Will Work for You.* The complete text of these confessions with their Scripture references can also be found in Charles Capps' book, *Faith and Confession,* (Tulsa, Oklahoma: Harrison House, 1987), pp. 307-315.

11

CONCLUSION: IT'S ONLY TEMPORARY

2 CORINTHIANS 4:8-18

The ultimate weapon against trouble is the knowledge that trouble is only temporary. No matter what the devil brings against us, *it is subject to change!* The apostle Paul had more trouble during his ministry than most of us can even imagine. But Paul was not troubled by his trouble because he knew the trouble was only temporary. And he knew he had a shield against trouble which would *never* fail him, the Word of God.

Let's see how Paul troubled his trouble, starting with verse 8 of 2 Corinthians 4:

> **We are troubled on every side, yet not distressed; we are perplexed, but not in despair;**
>
> **Persecuted, but not forsaken; cast down, but not destroyed;**
>
> **Always bearing about in the body the dying of the Lord Jesus, that the life also of Jesus might be made manifest in our body.**
>
> vv. 8-10

Now we know **in the beginning was the Word, and the Word was with God, and the Word was God.... And the Word was made flesh...** (John 1:1, 14). Therefore, instead of using "Jesus" now, I'm going to use "the Word of God."

Let me read verses 10 and 11 this way, so you can see what he's saying.

> **Always bearing about in the body the dying of the Lord Jesus, that the life also of *the Word of God* might be made manifest in our bodies.**

> **For we which live are alway delivered unto death for Jesus' sake, that the life also of *the Word of God* might be made manifest in our mortal flesh.**

Paul continues in verse 16:

> **For which cause we faint not...**

What cause? The life that's in the Word. In other words, "for which cause we don't faint, give up, cave in and quit."

> **...But though our outward man perish, yet the inward man is renewed day by day.**

> v. 16

Trouble in my way? That's all right, my inward man is being renewed day by day. When I got up this morning, I had a renewed inward man. Tomorrow I'll have a renewed inward man. The next day I'll have a renewed inward man. The day that I don't renew my inward man is the day that I'll be susceptible to the trouble in this world.

But look at Paul's attitude towards affliction.

> **For our light affliction...**

> v. 17

Look what Paul called *light affliction.* He calls a shipwreck *light affliction.* Being thrown in jail *light affliction.* Being whipped with a whip a *light affliction.*

For our light affliction, which is but for a moment...

v. 17

Only Temporary

How long was this moment? It doesn't matter. No matter how long it was, Paul says it was only temporary.

For our light affliction, which is but for a moment, worketh for us a far more exceeding and eternal weight of glory;

While we look not at the things which are seen, but at the things which are not seen: for the things which are seen are temporal; but the things which are not seen are eternal.

vv. 17,18

Things **which are seen** means things comprehended with our physical senses, things which can be picked up by our sensory mechanisms. And these things are what? *They're temporal!* They're so temporal. They're temporary.

In the Past

How many of you had a problem five years ago? Have you still got it? The doggone thing is gone, isn't it?

How many of you have ever been depressed? Are you depressed now? The thing changed, didn't it? It's subject to change.

How many of you have been broke before? Changed, didn't it? *Whatever you are going through, whatever you have been through, it is subject to change! It won't last always!*

That's why you ought to laugh at the devil! Whatever he's trying to do to you right now, you need to just tell him, "This is just temporary, boy." You need to remind the devil, "Hey, you do know this is going to change, don't you, ol' buddy?"

Subject to Change!

Somebody says, "I've got sickness on my body!" *Don't get upset! It's just a temporary thing!* This, too, must pass! You understand? If everything else in your past is in your past, then this is going to go where all of that stuff is in your past! Why? *It is subject to change!*

Somebody says, "Well, you know, I've got problems in my marriage!" Subject to change! "My wife nags!" Subject to change! "My husband's lazy!" Subject to change! "I don't have a job." Subject to change! "I'm not making enough money!" Subject to change! "I don't feel good." Subject to change! "I just don't know." Subject to change! Subject to change!

I don't care what it is, it's subject to change! It's subject to change!

"I don't know what the Lord put me on this earth for." Stay in the Word. The situation is subject to change. "Doesn't seem like God answers my prayers." Subject to change. You're going around letting a temporary something affect you for half your life. Subject to change. Oh, my goodness, subject to change. Subject to change.

Those Eternal Things

But those eternal things, the Word of God, are not temporary, they're eternal. And eternal things will affect temporary things.

What determines whether a thing is temporary? *When it's not absolute Bible truth.* It can be a *fact,* but if it's not Bible truth, it can be changed.

Do you want an example? The doctor says you've got cancer. But because that isn't what the Word says, that isn't the truth. Therefore, you say, "All right, God, I'm going to get the truth. By His stripes I'm healed." That truth changes a fact! So that makes cancer temporary. So why are you afraid of it? It won't be there but a little while anyway. Don't let cancer convince you that it's powerful, and don't put confidence in its ability because it's just temporary. So if some of you are suffering from sickness and disease, remember it's temporary! It has to go, and you don't have to go with it.

Whatever you're going through, it's temporary. It's only for a moment. Praise the Lord!

Be Not Troubled

Child of God, just because trouble comes, it doesn't have to overcome. You don't have to be troubled by trouble. You can trouble your trouble with the Word of God. As a born-again child of God, as an heir of *soteria,* you aren't of the system of this world. Therefore, you don't have to operate according to the system of this world. You can have peace because you can operate according to the system of God's Word!

Remember our Savior's powerful words:

These things I have spoken unto you, that in me ye might have peace. In the world ye shall have tribulation: but be of good cheer; I have overcome the world.

JOHN 16:33

Dr. Creflo A. Dollar Jr. is pastor and founder of World Changers Church International, a non-denominational church located in College Park, Georgia.

Formerly an educational therapist, Creflo Dollar began the ministry in 1986 with eight people. He is now an international teacher and conference speaker with a congregation of over seventeen thousand people.

Creflo Dollar has been called of God to teach the gospel with simplicity and understanding. He can be seen and heard throughout the world on "Changing Your World" broadcasts via television and radio.

For a brochure of books and tapes
by Dr. Creflo A. Dollar Jr., write:
World Changers Church International
P. O. Box 490124
College Park, Georgia 30349
*Please include your prayer requests and comments
when you write.*

OTHER BOOKS BY CREFLO A. DOLLAR JR.

The Color of Love:
Understanding God's Answer to Racism,
Separation and Division

Answers Awaiting in the Presence of God

Uprooting the Spirit of Fear

Available from your local bookstore.

HARRISON HOUSE
Tulsa, Oklahoma 74153

THE HARRISON HOUSE VISION

Proclaiming the truth and the power

Of the Gospel of Jesus Christ

With excellence;

Challenging Christians to

Live victoriously,

Grow spiritually,

Know God intimately.